A Puzzling Tour of India

yali books

Published by Yali Books, New York

Text and Illustrations copyright © 2016 by Ambika Sambasivan

All rights reserved. No part of this book may be reproduced or transmitted in any form or by any means, electronic or mechanical, including photocopying, recording, or by any information storage and retrieval system, without the written permission of the publisher.

Connect with us online -

www.yalibooks.com
www.facebook.com/YaliBooks
www.twitter.com/YaliBooks

ISBN: 978-0-98-906152-0

Welcome to incredible India!

Before you begin your journey through this fascinating sub-continent, we need to make sure you are ready. Make your way through this twisty map to warm up your puzzling skills. Ready, set, go!

Mumbai's biggest flea market, Chor Bazaar, is stocked with old and strange-looking objects. Can you sort through the jumble to find these eight things?

- a goat
- a genie's lamp
- a set of balance scales
- a pencil
- a paper fan
- a spear
- a megaphone
- a bicycle wheel

Today is Uttarayan in Gujarat – a day for eating delicious 'puri-undhiyo' and flying kites.

Oh dear! Ram, Devi, Ravi and Neha seem to have got their kites entangled. Can you help them sort it out by tracing each kite back to its owner?

Can you find your way through Ahmedabad's Old City?

Start at the produce market, the first landmark on your route. Work your way across the city to Ellis Bridge (2), zoom past Bhadra Kila (3) and Teen Darwaza (4), stop at Jama Masjid (5), and breeze past Manek Chowk (6) and Rangila Pol (7) to finally exit through Dilli Darwaza (8).

We are at Ahmedabad's crowded Teen Darwaza market. Here is a shopping list of the things we want but we need your help to find them –

a potato
an onion
a pumpkin
a tomato
an okra
an orange slice
a gherkin
a banana pepper
a slice of watermelon
a cauliflower

My! Look at all the different kinds of turbans, caps and mustaches! Only two of these men are identical. Can you find them?

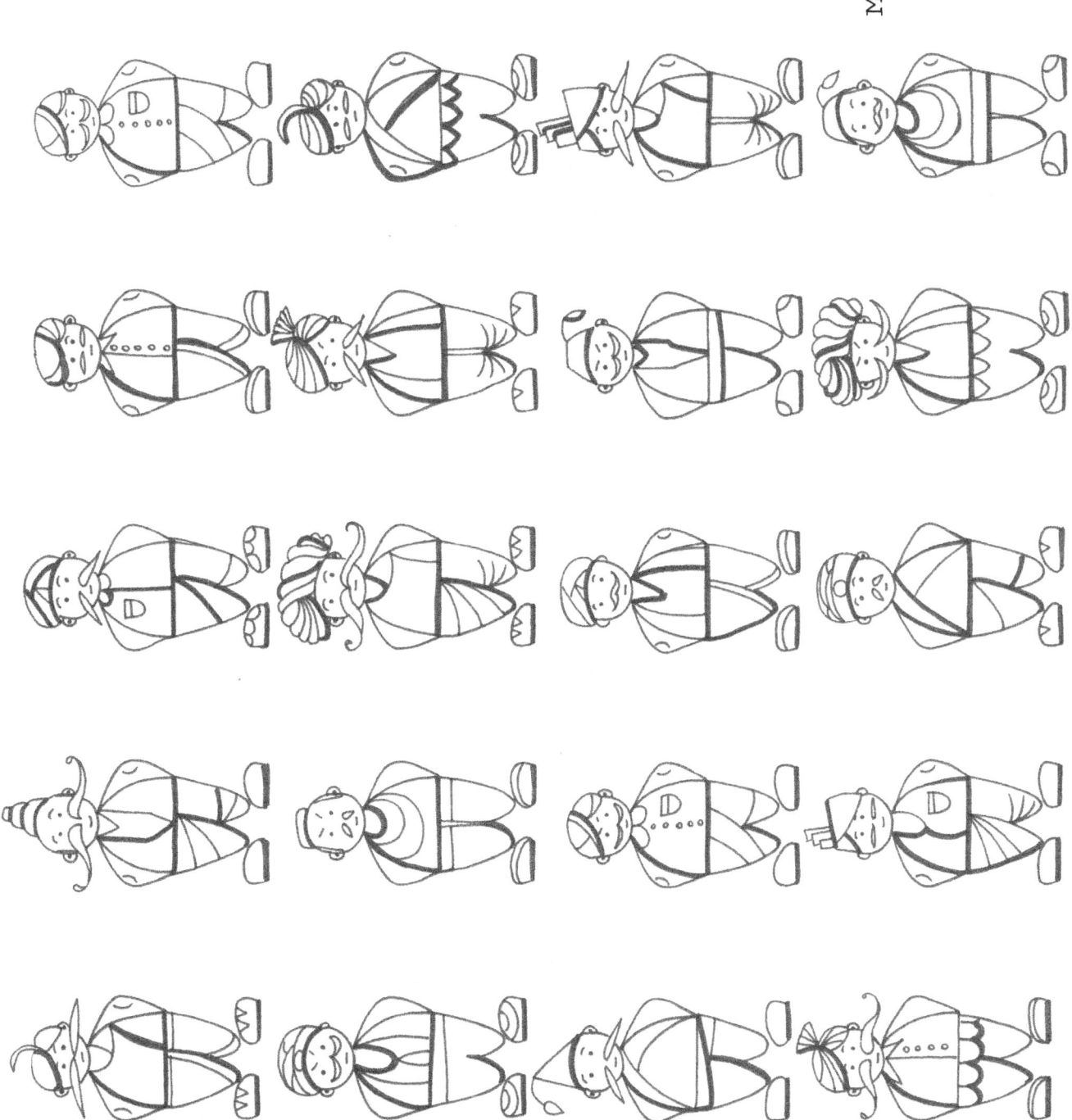

A tourist took these two pictures of the Maharajah of Jaipur on his morning walk. The pictures are identical except for ten tiny differences. Can you find them?

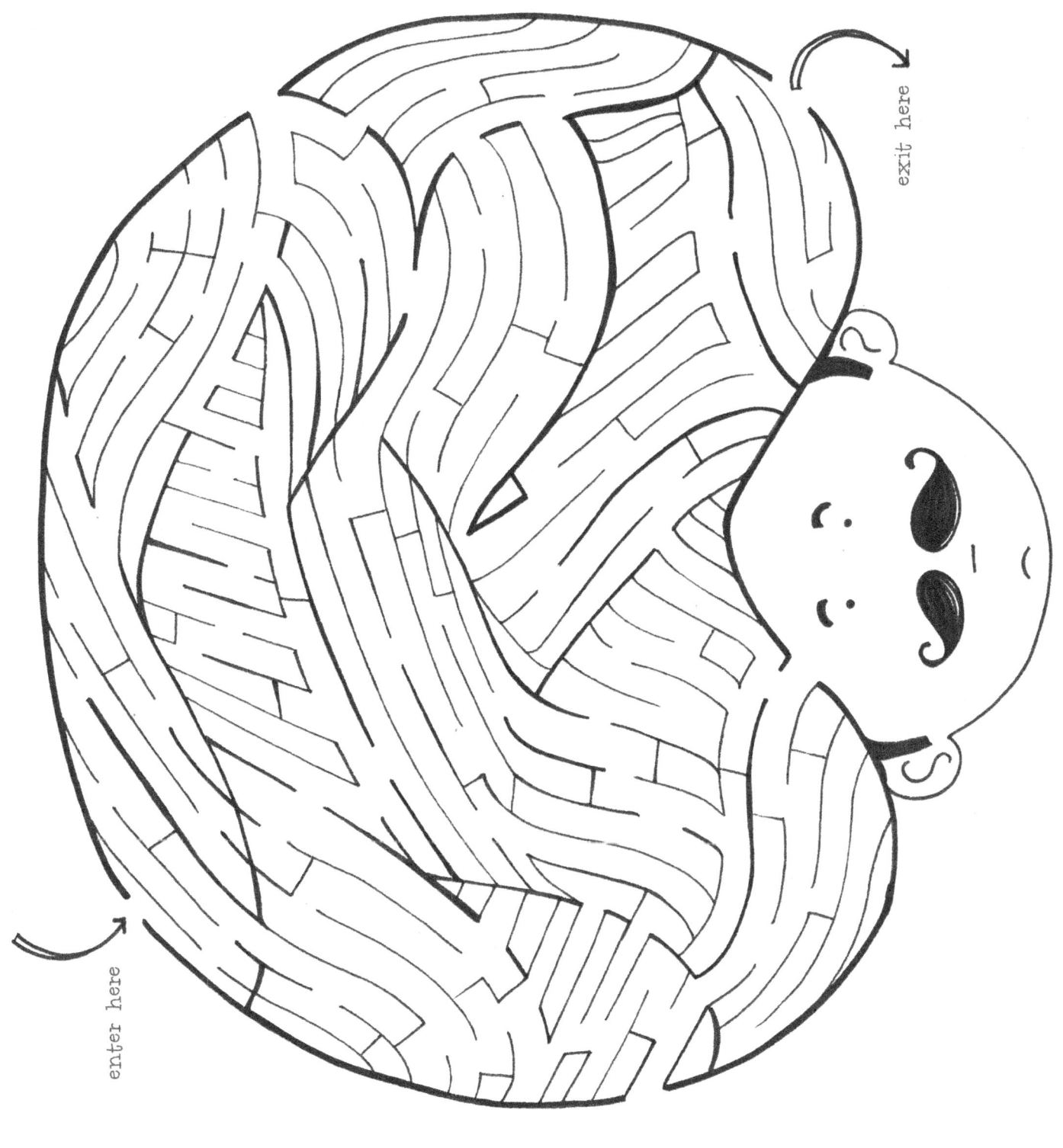

This Rajasthani farmer is wearing a special turban called a "leheriya pagadi", which is tied with a very long piece of cloth. Can you find your way out through all its folds and pleats?

Hidden in this picture of the famous Taj Mahal are ten mangoes that look like this - ◯.

Can you find them all?

When you are done, 'take' a selfie in front of the Taj. Just draw your picture in the box on the left and show it off to all your friends!

Connect the dots to reveal Jim Corbett National Park's most famous resident. Don't be afraid, it is only a puzzle!

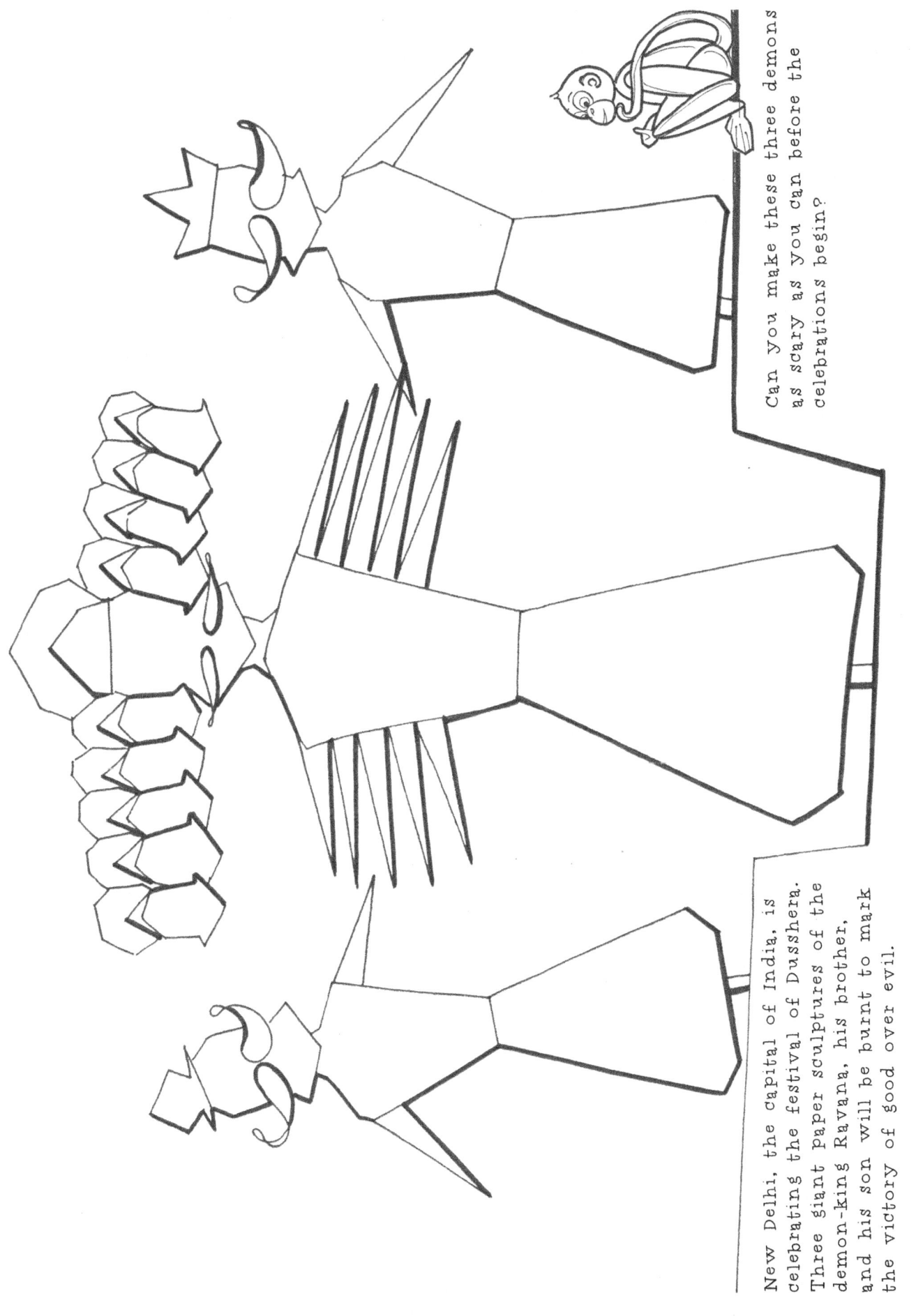

New Delhi, the capital of India, is celebrating the festival of Dusshera. Three giant paper sculptures of the demon-king Ravana, his brother, and his son will be burnt to mark the victory of good over evil.

Can you make these three demons as scary as you can before the celebrations begin?

Traveling around New Delhi, we spotted this sandstone and marble tower that is over 800 years old and 22 stories tall. Can you figure out what it is called? Use the first letter of the name of each object in the boxes below to spell out the name of this monument.

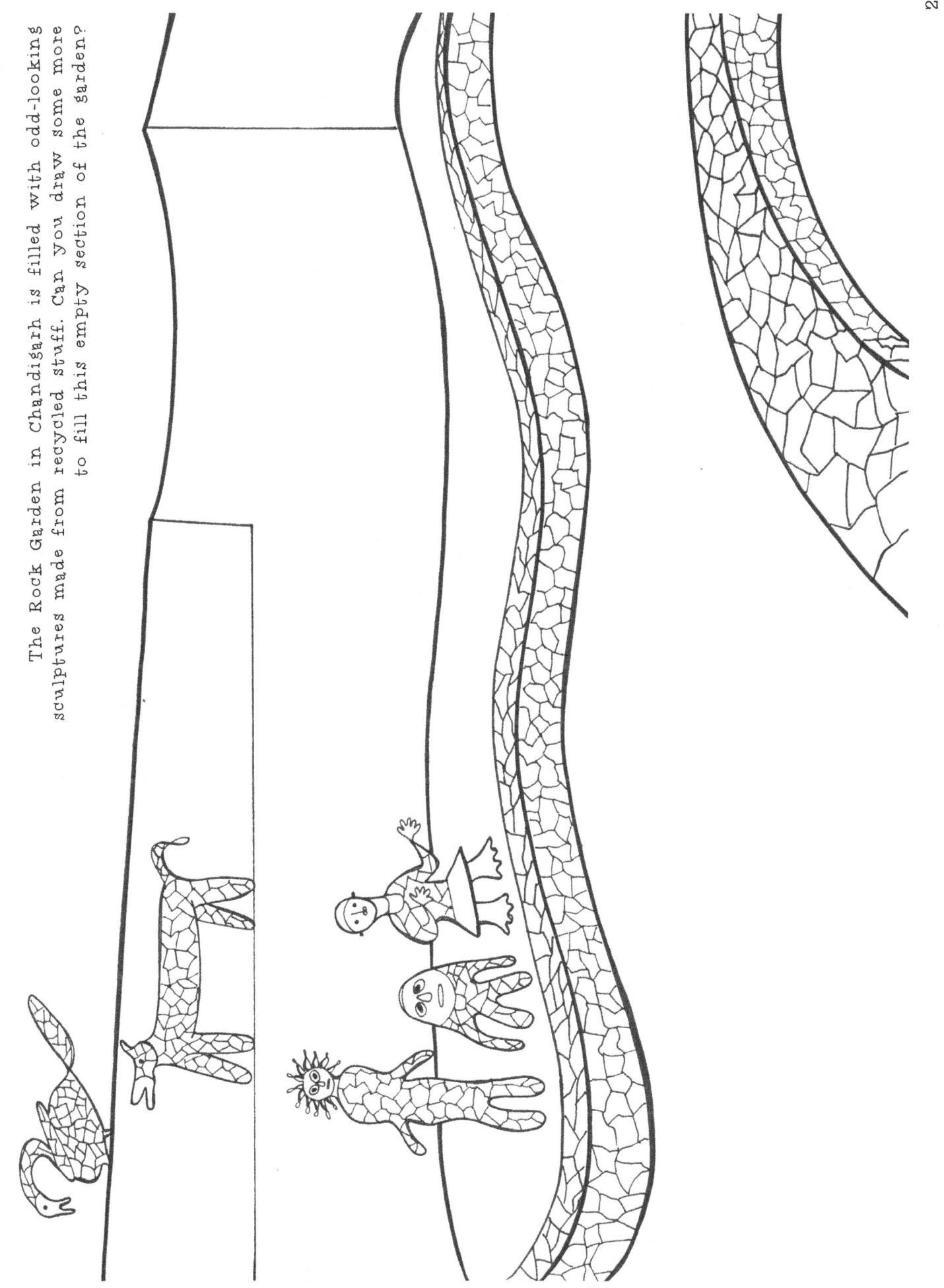

Punjab is home to a great many sunflower fields, like the one in this puzzle. Can you find a path through the flowers and the odd tractor or two?

enter →

exit ↰

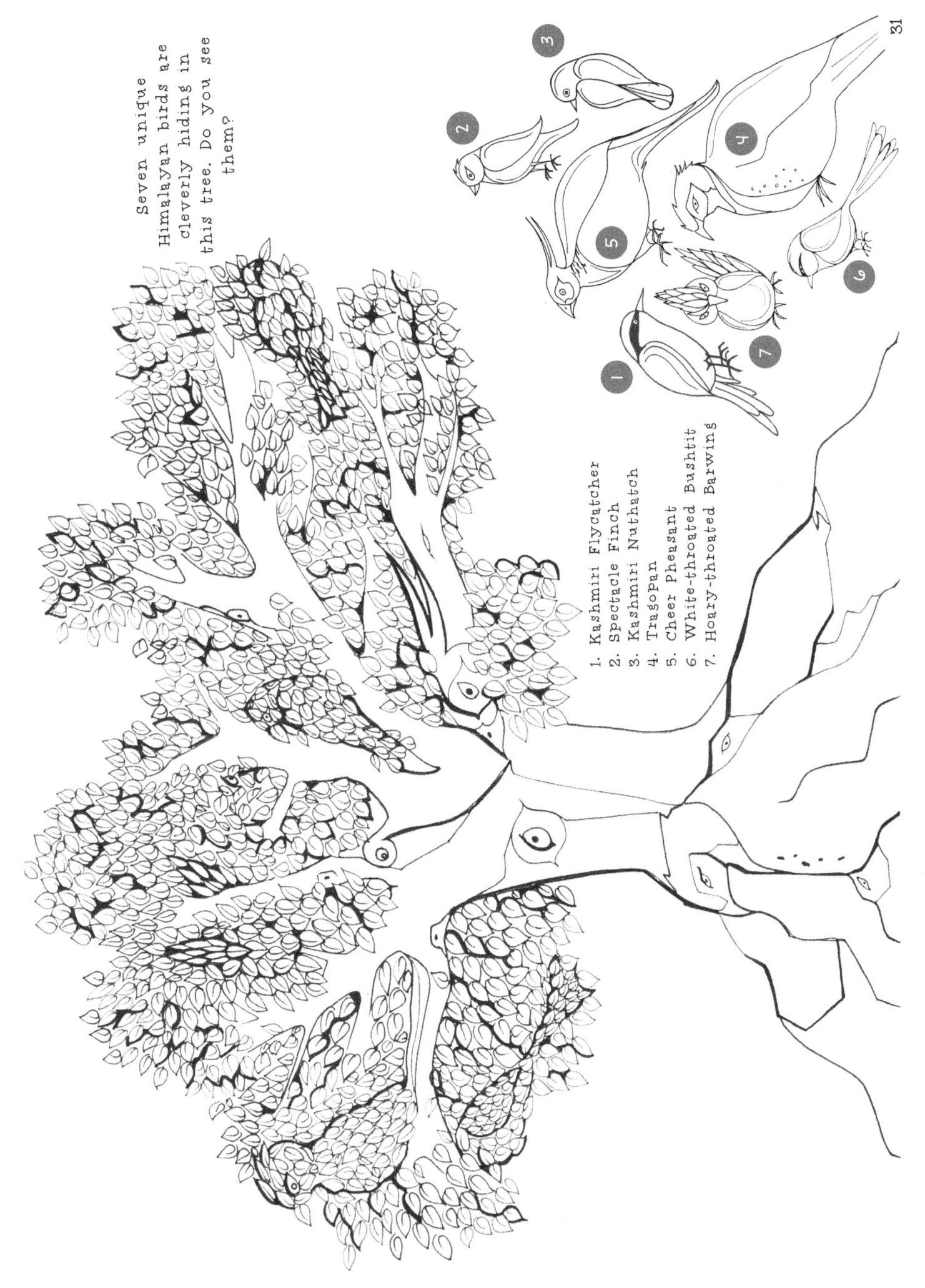

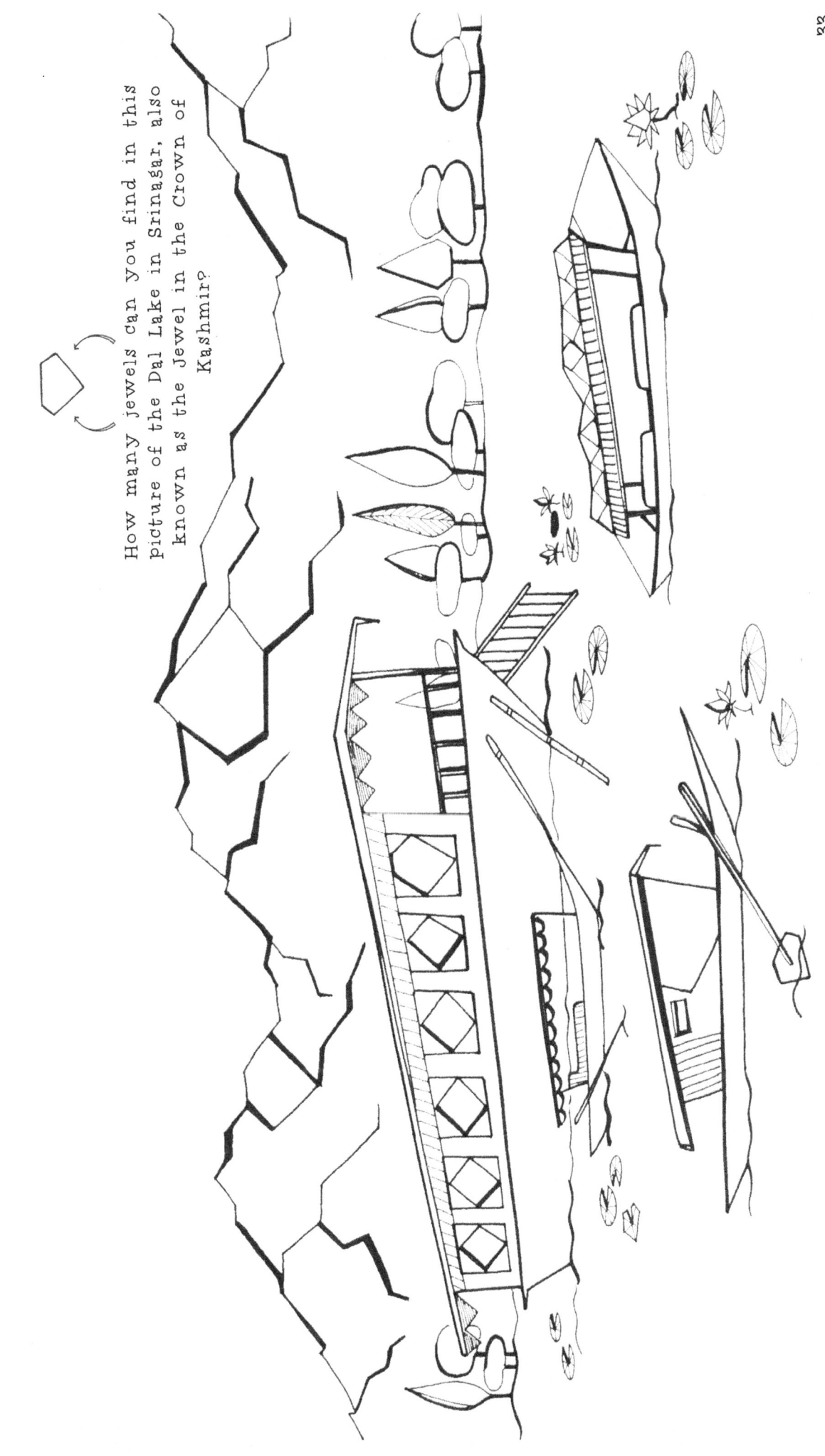

How many jewels can you find in this picture of the Dal Lake in Srinagar, also known as the Jewel in the Crown of Kashmir?

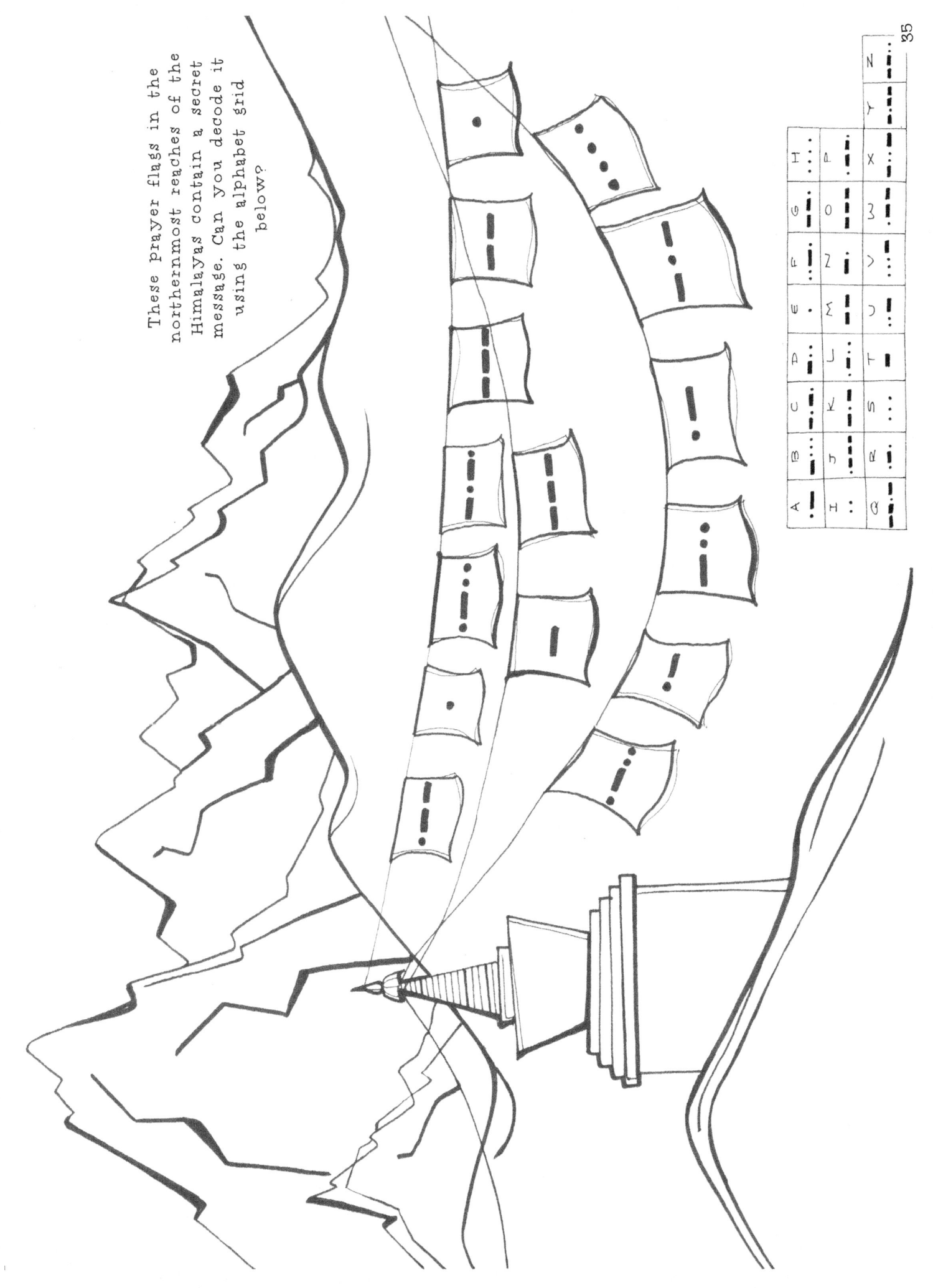

The river Ganga is home to the gharial, a unique member of the crocodile family. Very few are left in the wild, which is why this fellow needs your help.

Cut along the dotted lines and put the pieces back together to reveal one very hungry gharial and his soon-to-be dinner!

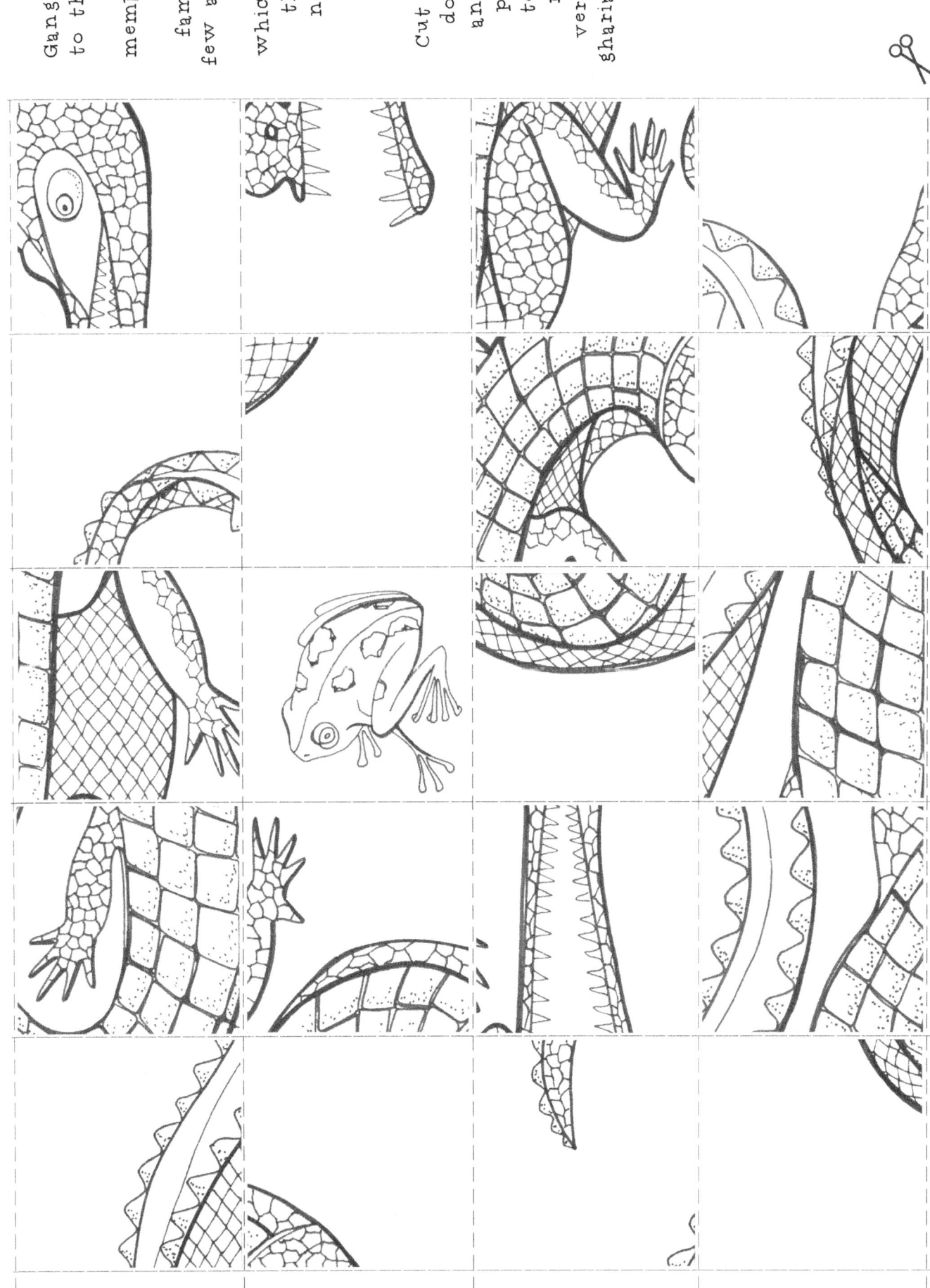

These two brothers have identical sweet shops in the bustling city of Lucknow, except for 12 tiny differences. How quickly can you spot them?

The banks of the River Ganga at Varanasi are teeming with activity...and the alphabet! Can you spot all the letters from A to Z in this picture?

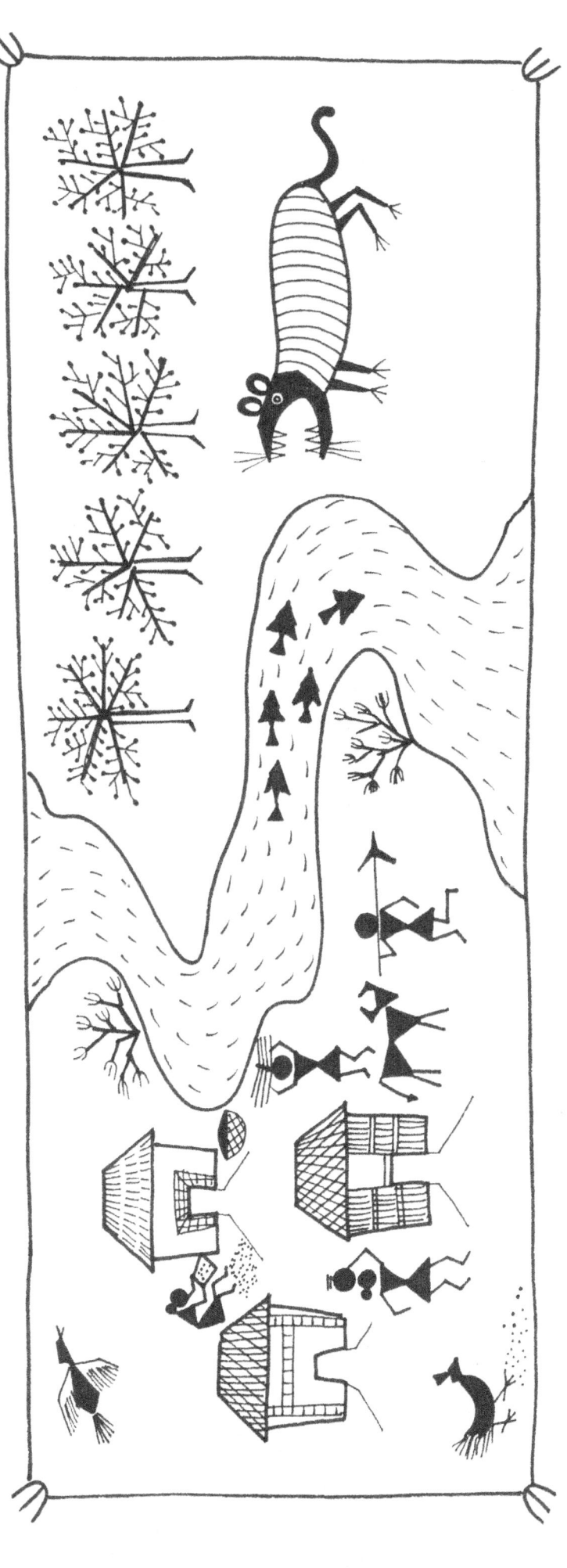

The Warli tribes
from the Sahyadri
Mountains in
Central India tell
stories through
their art. They use
rice paste to create
elaborate paintings
on the walls of
their homes. Can
you write a story
from the Warli
painting on this
page?

Early man created some of the first examples of art in India at the Bhimbetka Rock Caves in Madhya Pradesh. Some of these paintings are nearly 30,000 years old!

Now you can make your own cave art! Just draw these men around the bison in the marked positions to create a Paleolithic hunting scene.

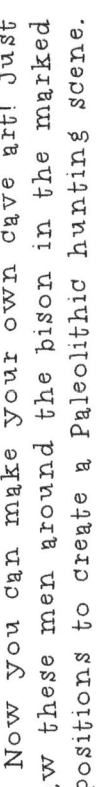
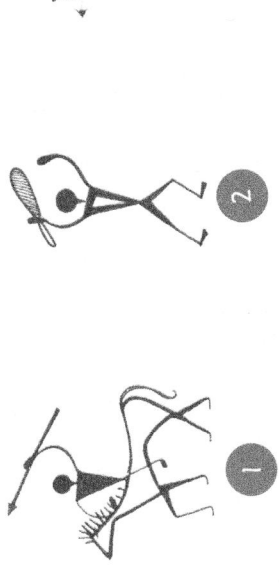
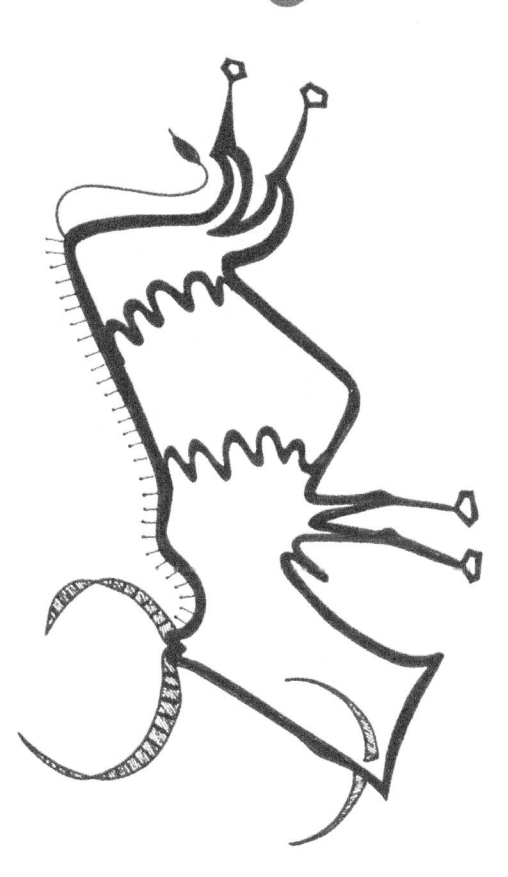

Delicious jackfruits hanging from trees are a common sight in Southern India. These fruits are humungous, some weigh up to 80 pounds!

Oh dear! One large fruit is coming down quite rapidly on a poor unsuspecting snail! Can you quickly sketch out a clever idea to save the snail?

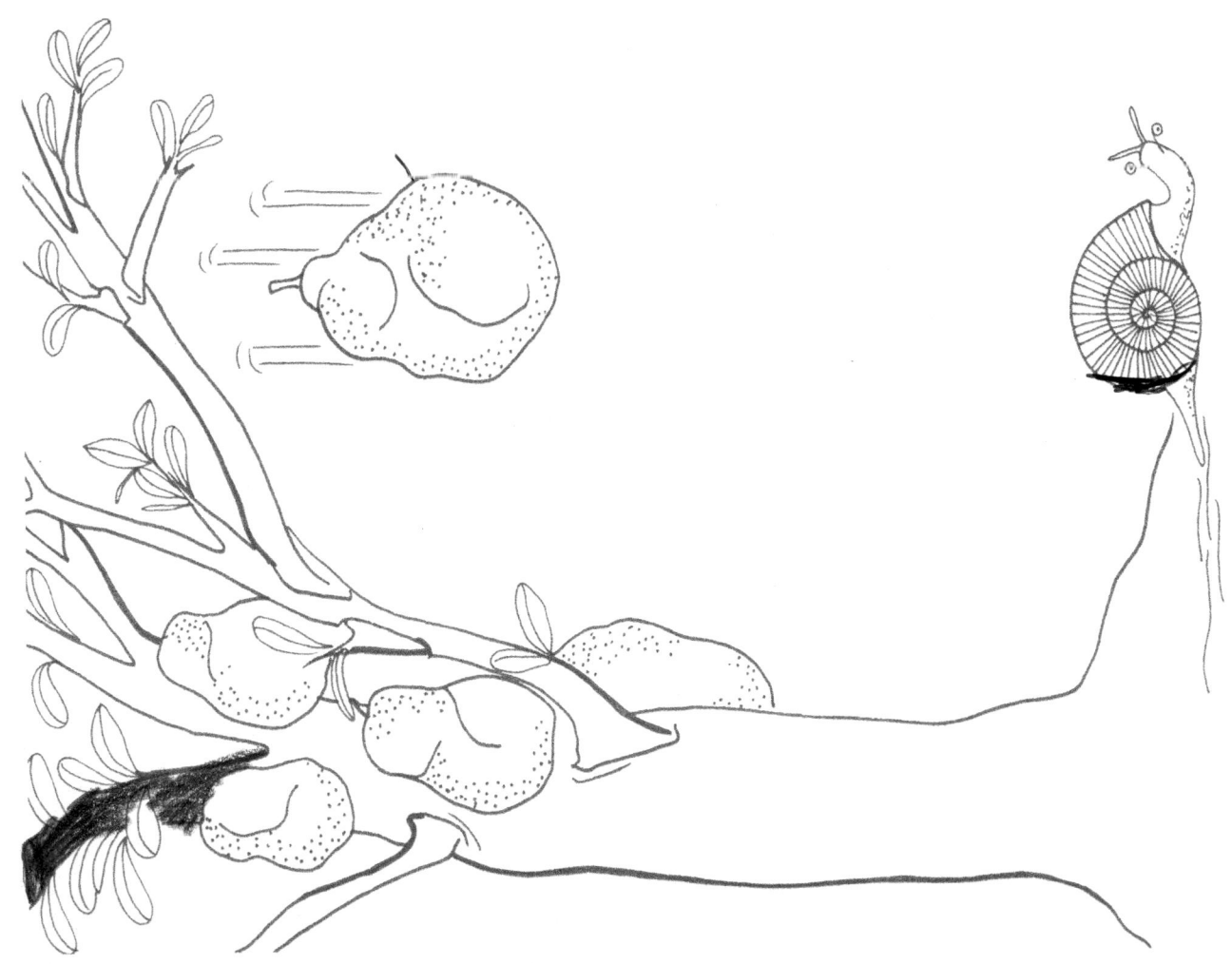

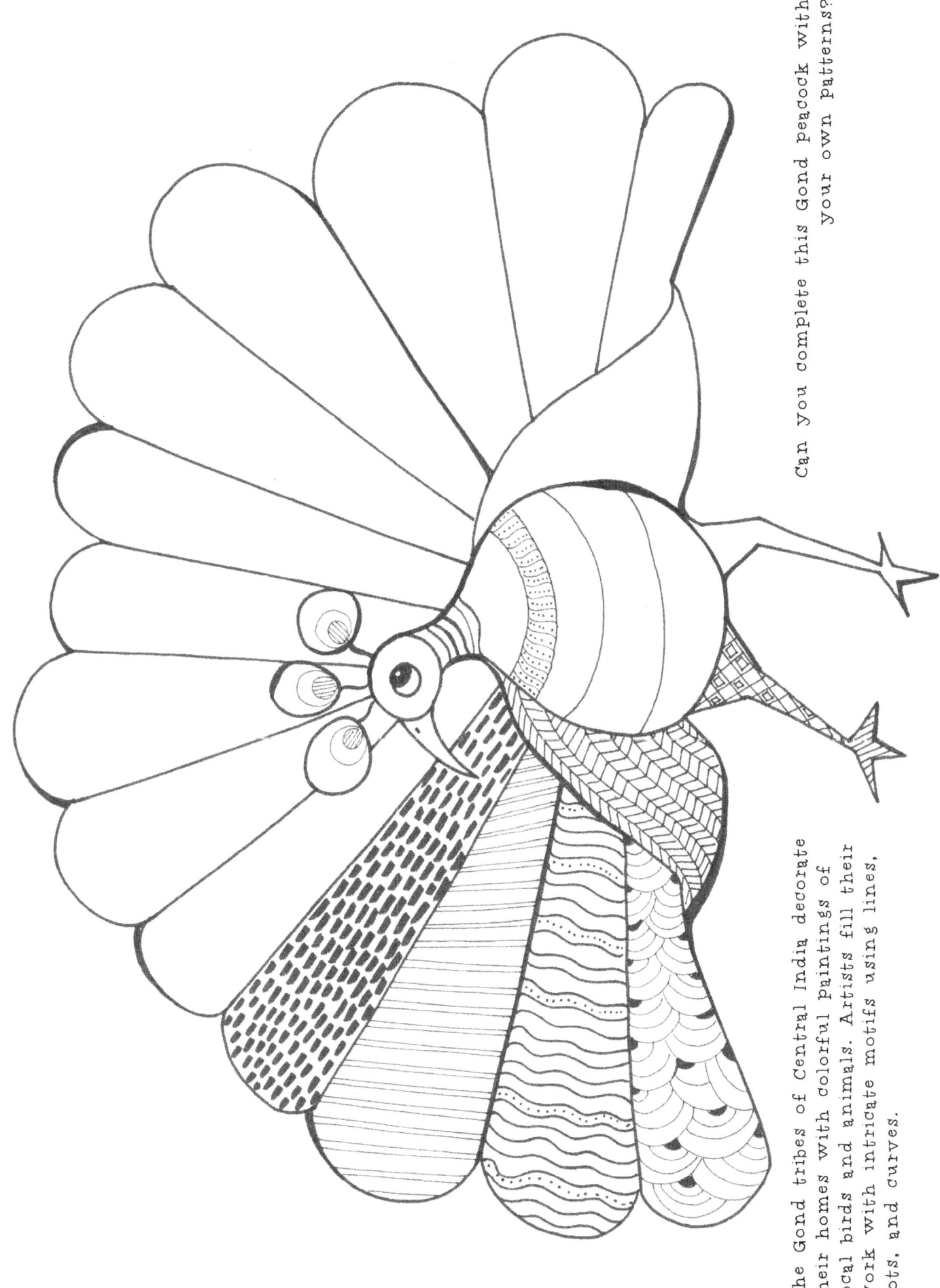

Can you complete this Gond peacock with your own patterns?

The Gond tribes of Central India decorate their homes with colorful paintings of local birds and animals. Artists fill their work with intricate motifs using lines, dots, and curves.

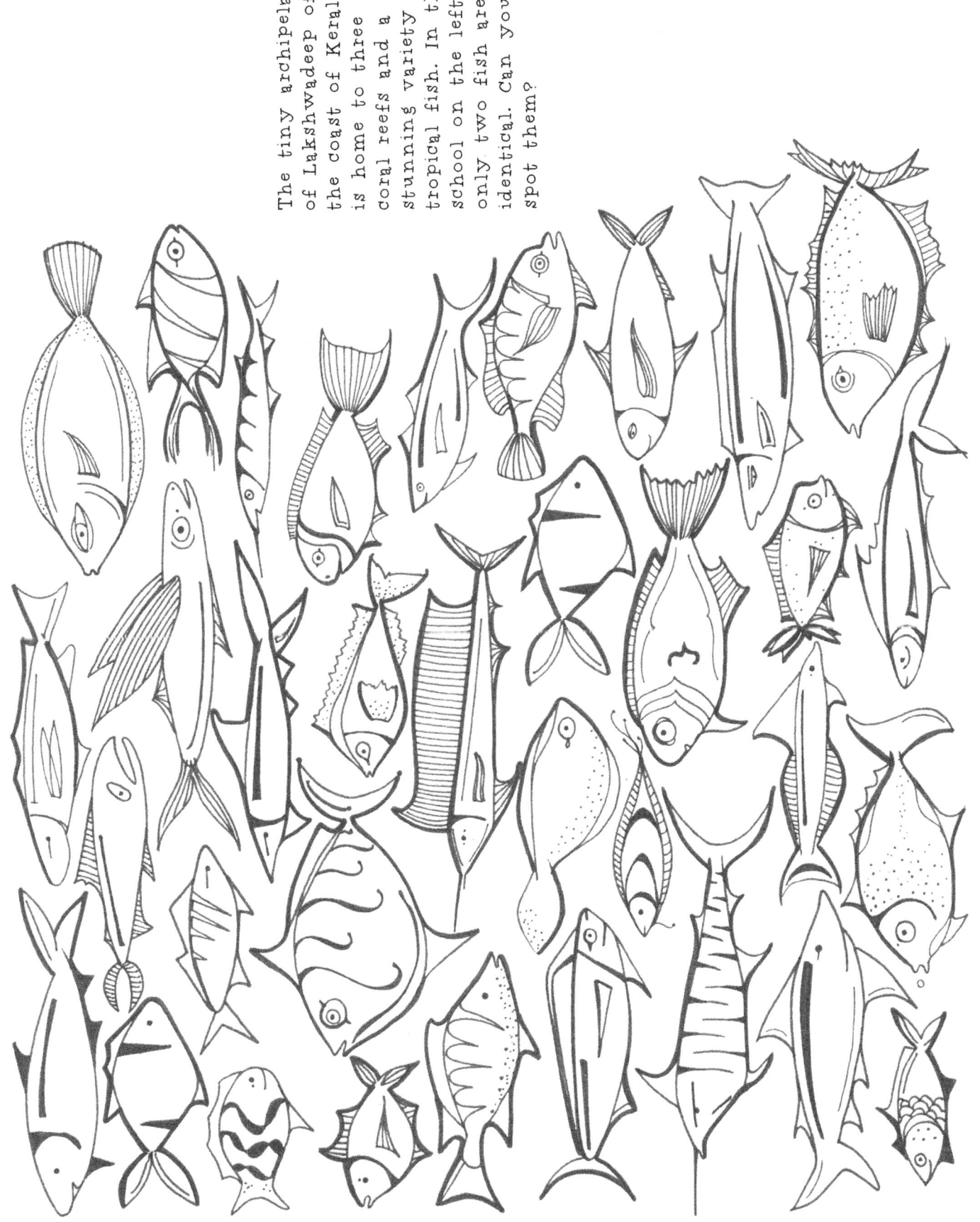

The tiny archipelago of Lakshwadeep off the coast of Kerala is home to three coral reefs and a stunning variety of tropical fish. In the school on the left, only two fish are identical. Can you spot them?

Did you know that India has its own forms of opera? Yakshagana is one such opera from coastal Karnataka. Actors use elaborate costumes and makeup to tell stories through dance and music.

Would you like to create your own Yakshagana drama? Just color the puppets on this page, cut them out and wrap them around your fingers. Make up a short story and stage a little play for your friends.

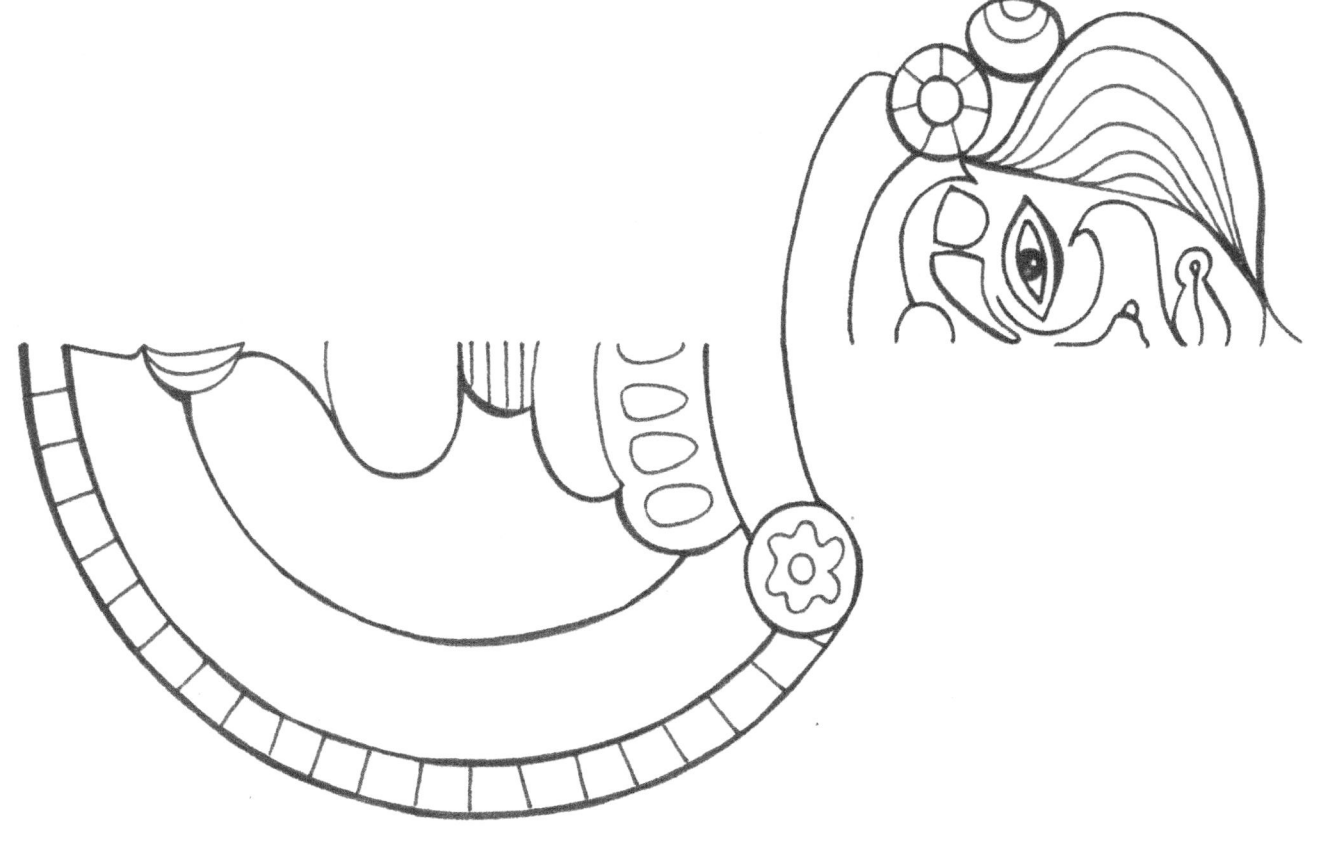

Can you help this Kathakali dancer get ready for his performance? You need to complete his face and headdress by copying the shapes from the other side to create a mirror image. Once you are done, make it as colorful as you can!

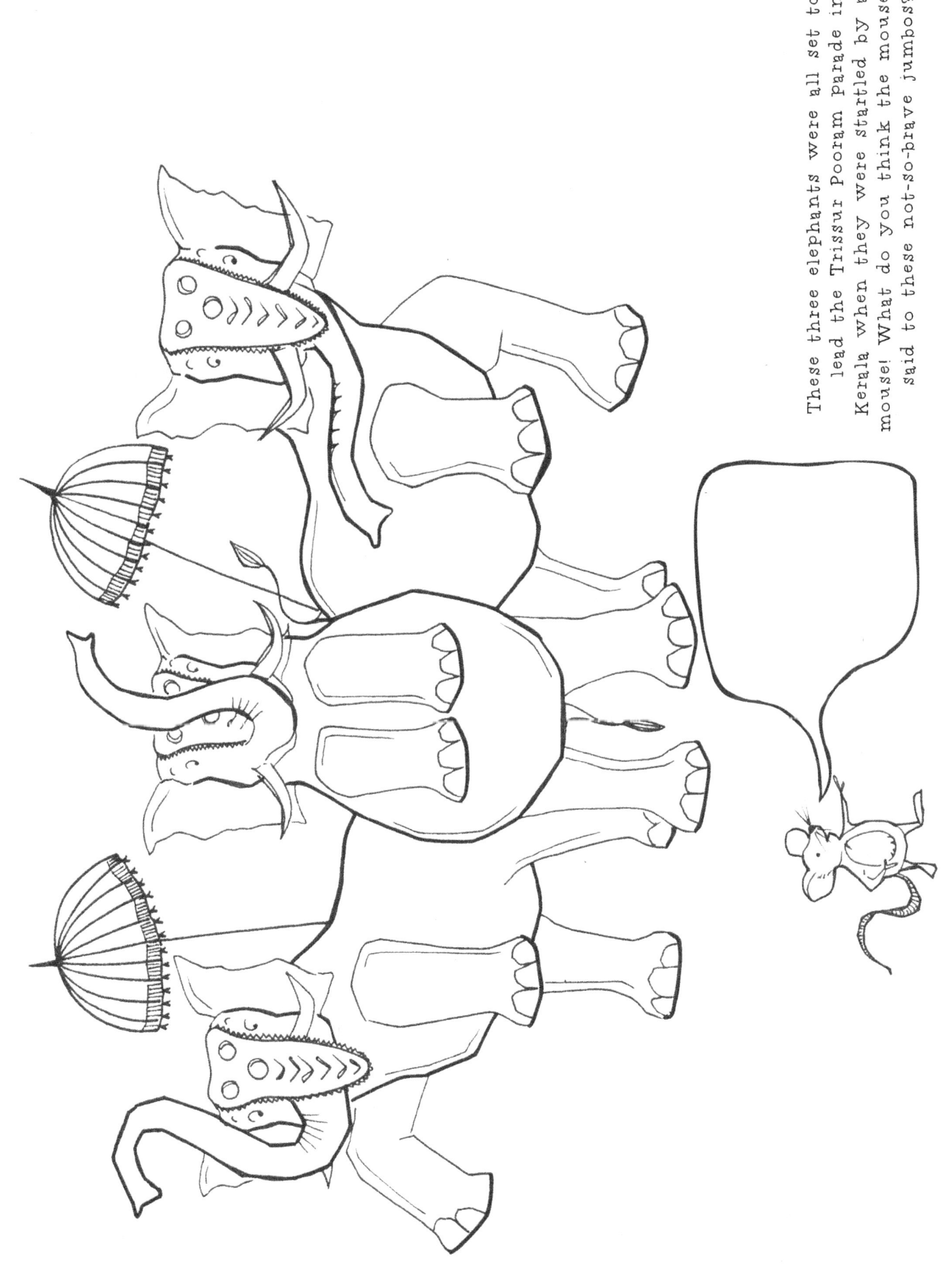

These three elephants were all set to lead the Trissur Pooram parade in Kerala when they were startled by a mouse! What do you think the mouse said to these not-so-brave jumbos?

Things seem to be a bit odd at the busy Charminar district in Hyderabad. Can you spot at least nine objects that are out of place in this scene?

It is the festival of Onam in Kerala and the great snake boat race, Vallam Kalli, is all set to begin. Each village sends a boat and a team of rowers to the race in the hope of winning the grand prize.

One boat, however, needs your puzzle-solving skills. Cut the pieces out and put the boat back together as quickly as you can. May the best team win!

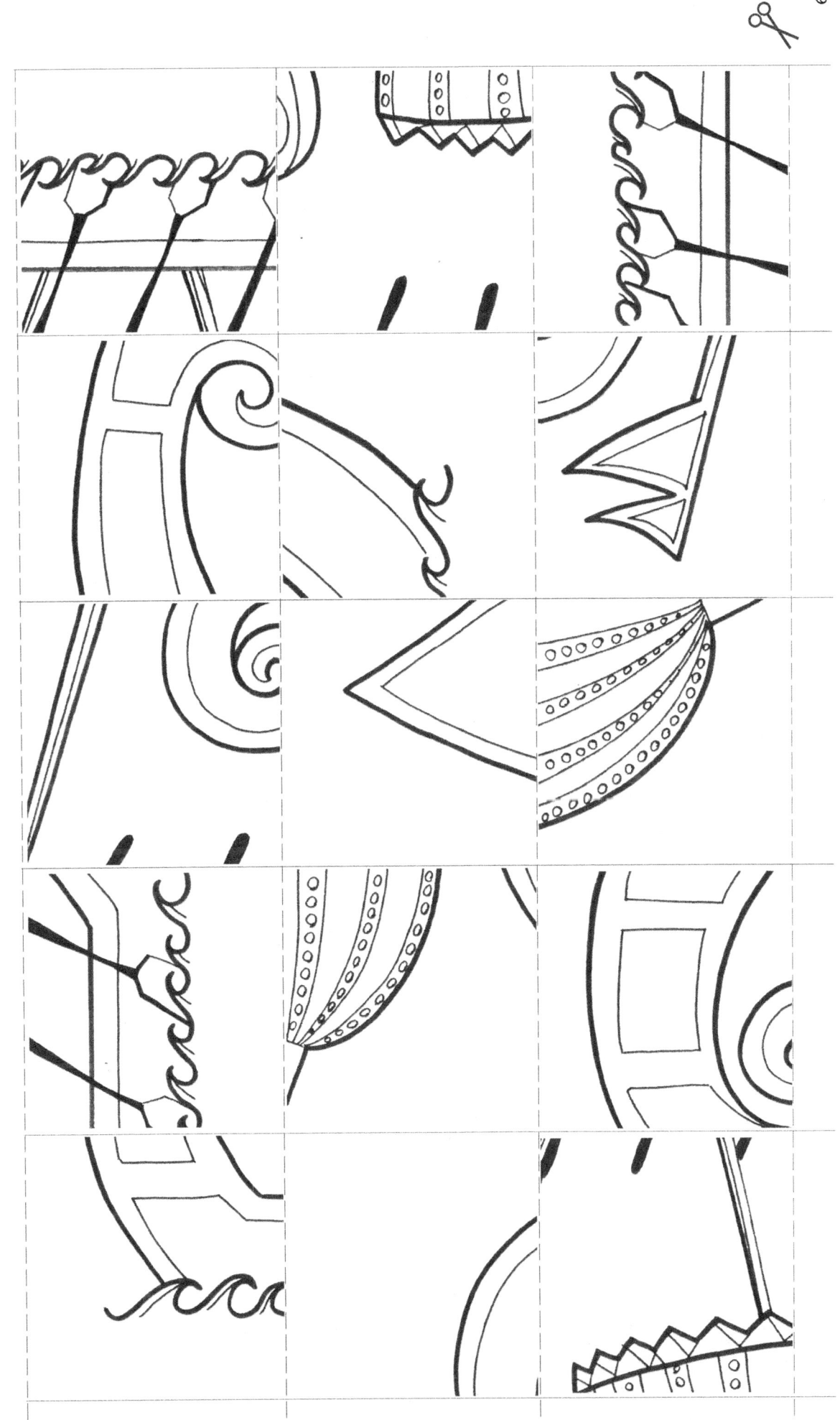

In Madurai, a group of dancers are wearing horse costumes for a Poikal Kudarai performance. The fourth man doesn't have a horse yet. Can you pick the right one from the six choices below?

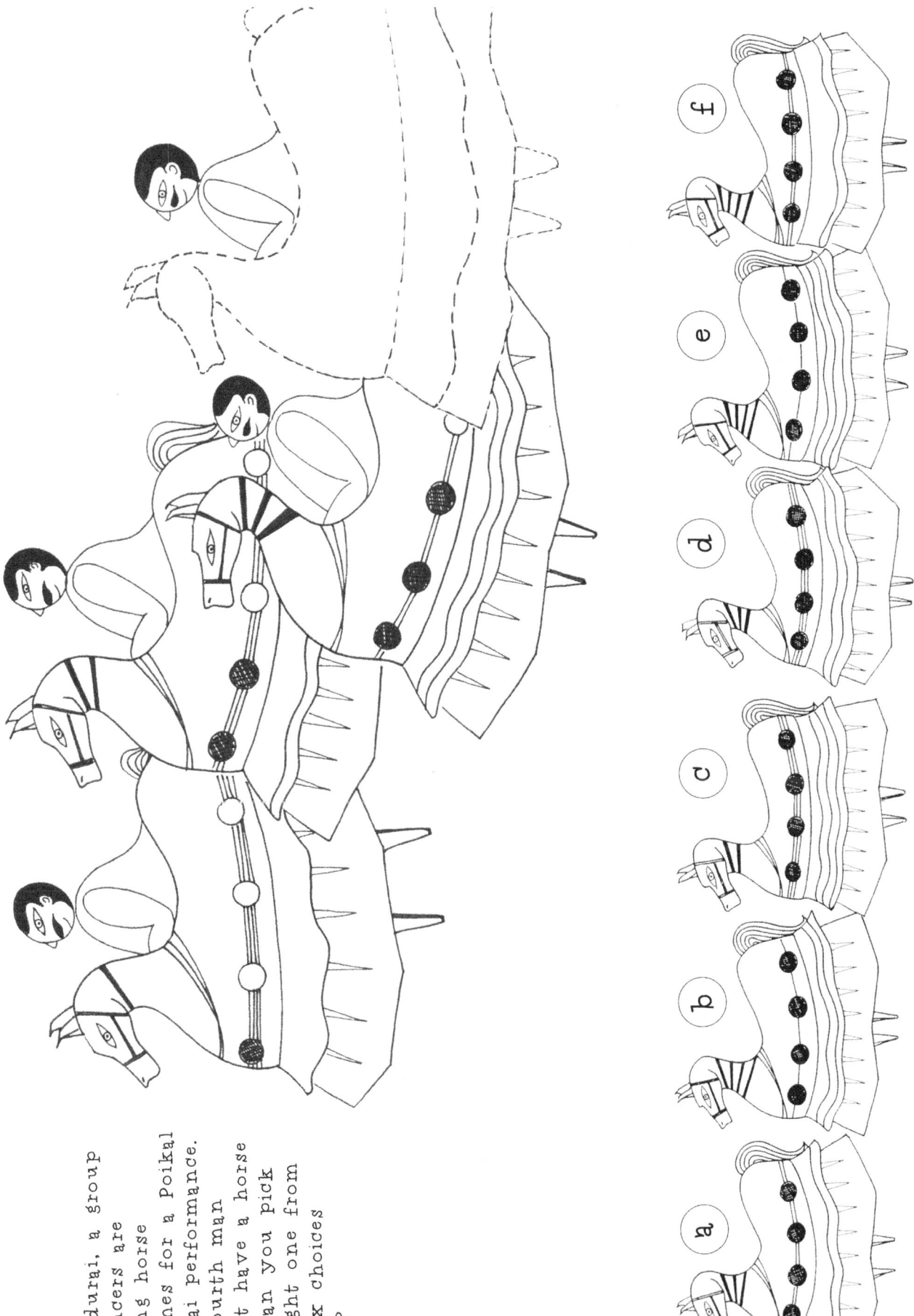

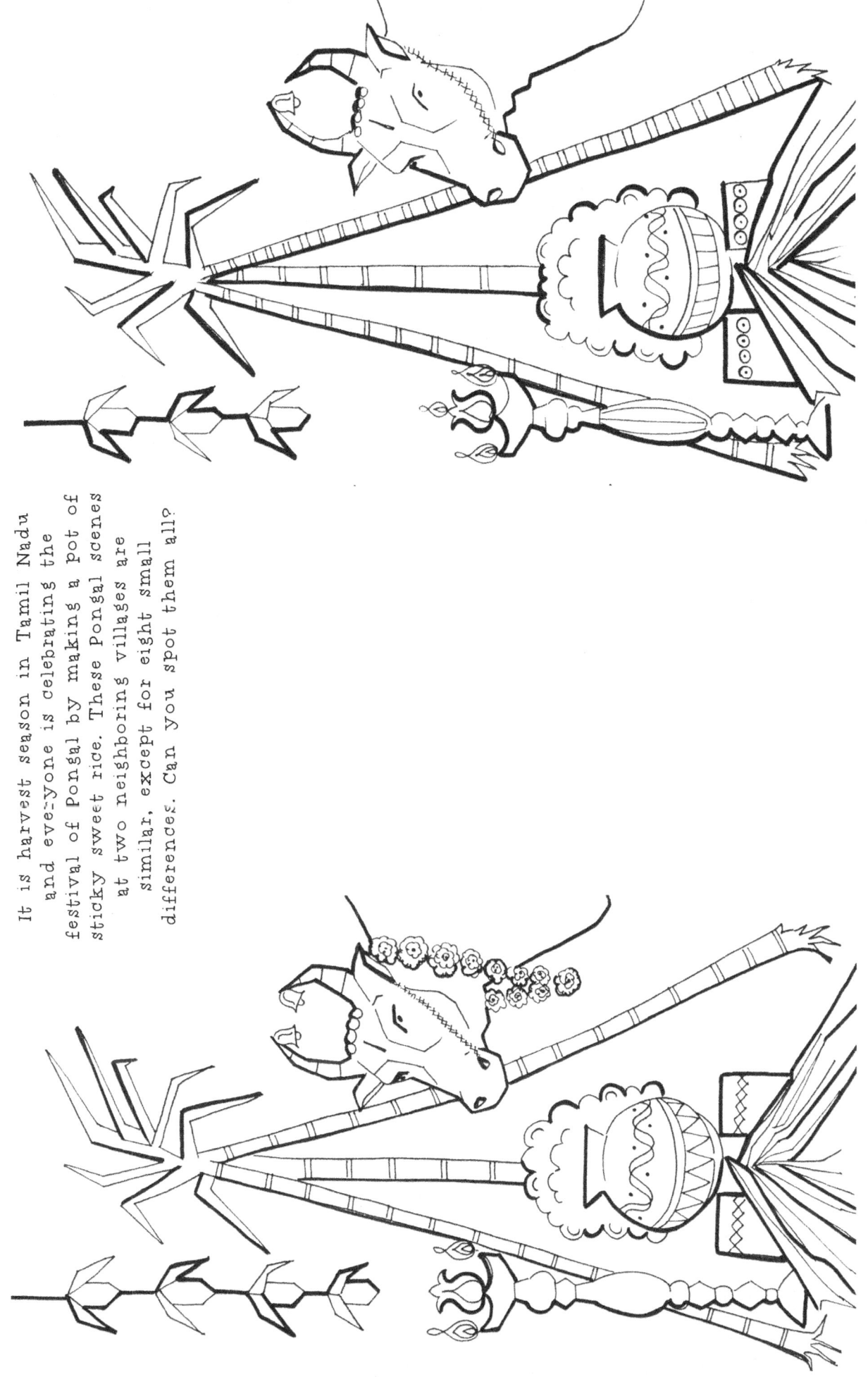

It is harvest season in Tamil Nadu and everyone is celebrating the festival of Pongal by making a pot of sticky sweet rice. These Pongal scenes at two neighboring villages are similar, except for eight small differences. Can you spot them all?

The grand Big Temple in Tanjavur is over a thousand years old. It is truly a very large temple. Its main tower or Vimana, is nearly 220 feet tall and the capstone right on top weighs 80 tons!

It is also easy to get lost here. Can you make your way through the temple, starting at the very top of the Vimana?

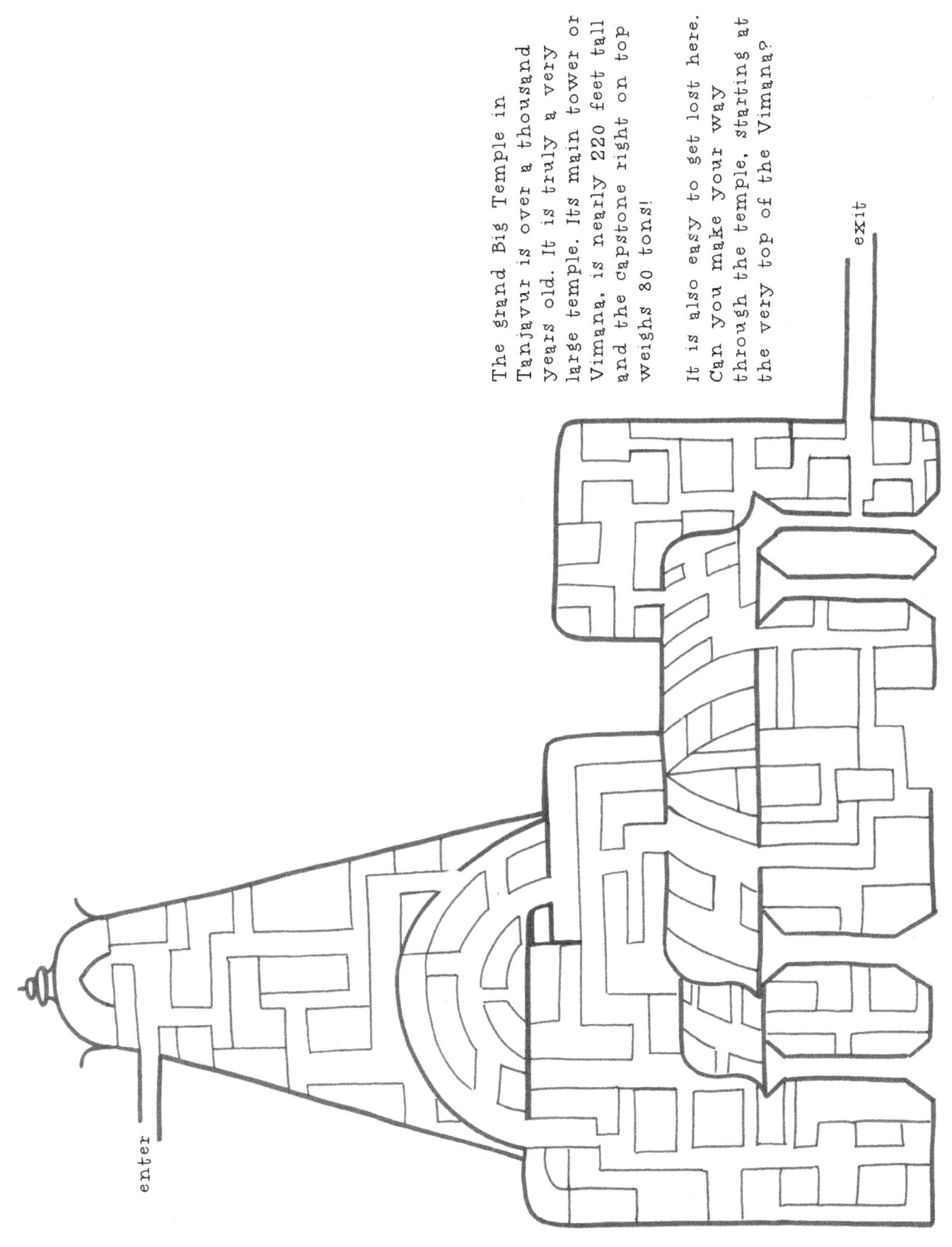

We are admiring the large collection of tropical plants and trees inside the Glass House at Lalbagh Botanical Gardens.

Can you figure out which city we are in? Find the letters hidden in the picture and unscramble them to get the answer.

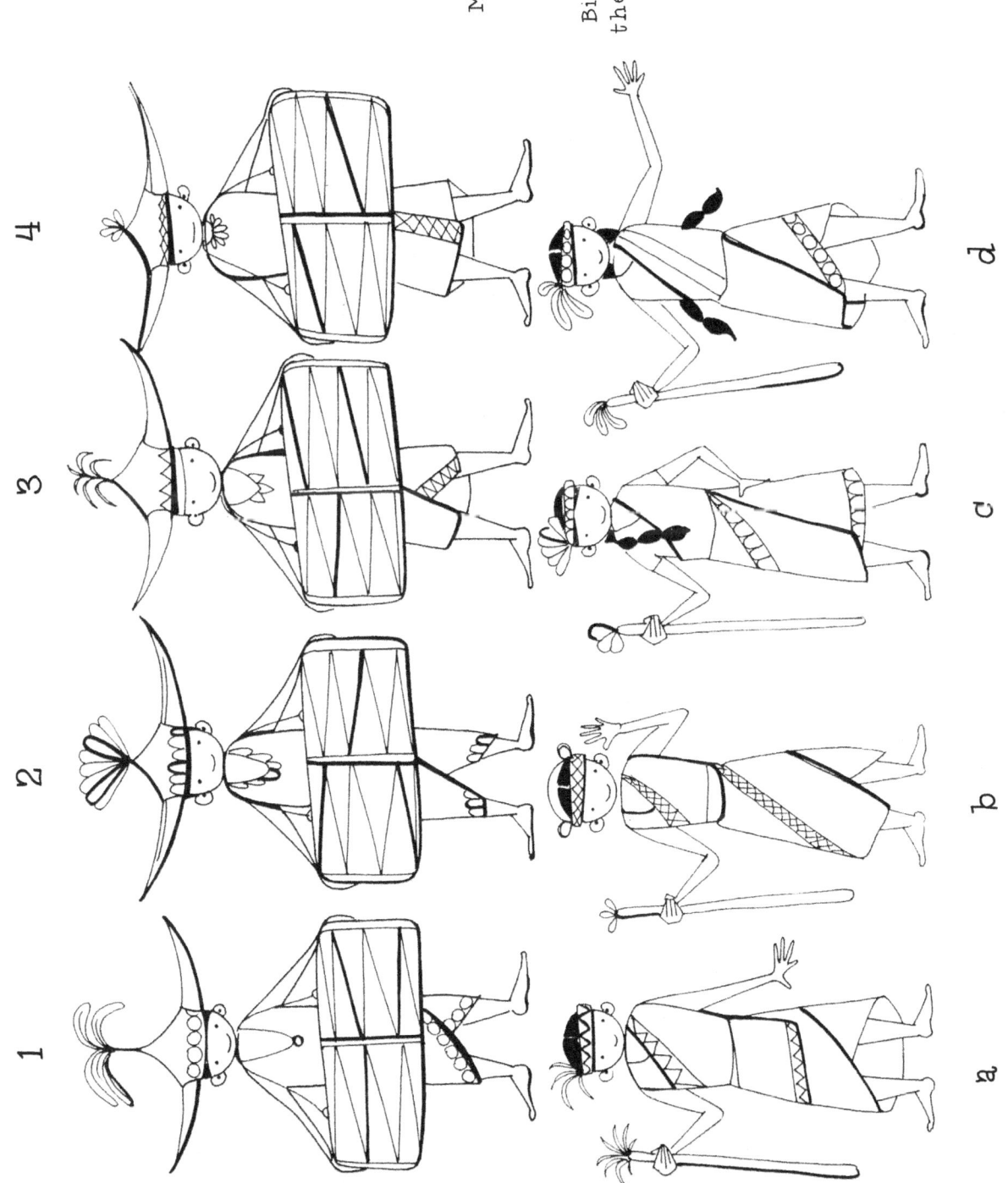

Men of the Sing Maria tribe in Madhya Pradesh are looking for dance partners for the traditional Gaur or Bison dance. Can you match them up with the women in the second row?

Even the gods have family to visit. The deities at the Jagannath Temple in Puri travel in giant chariots to visit their relatives every year during a nine-day trip called Rath Yatra.

A few pieces are missing in this picture of the Yatra. Can you match the pieces below to the gaps in the picture?

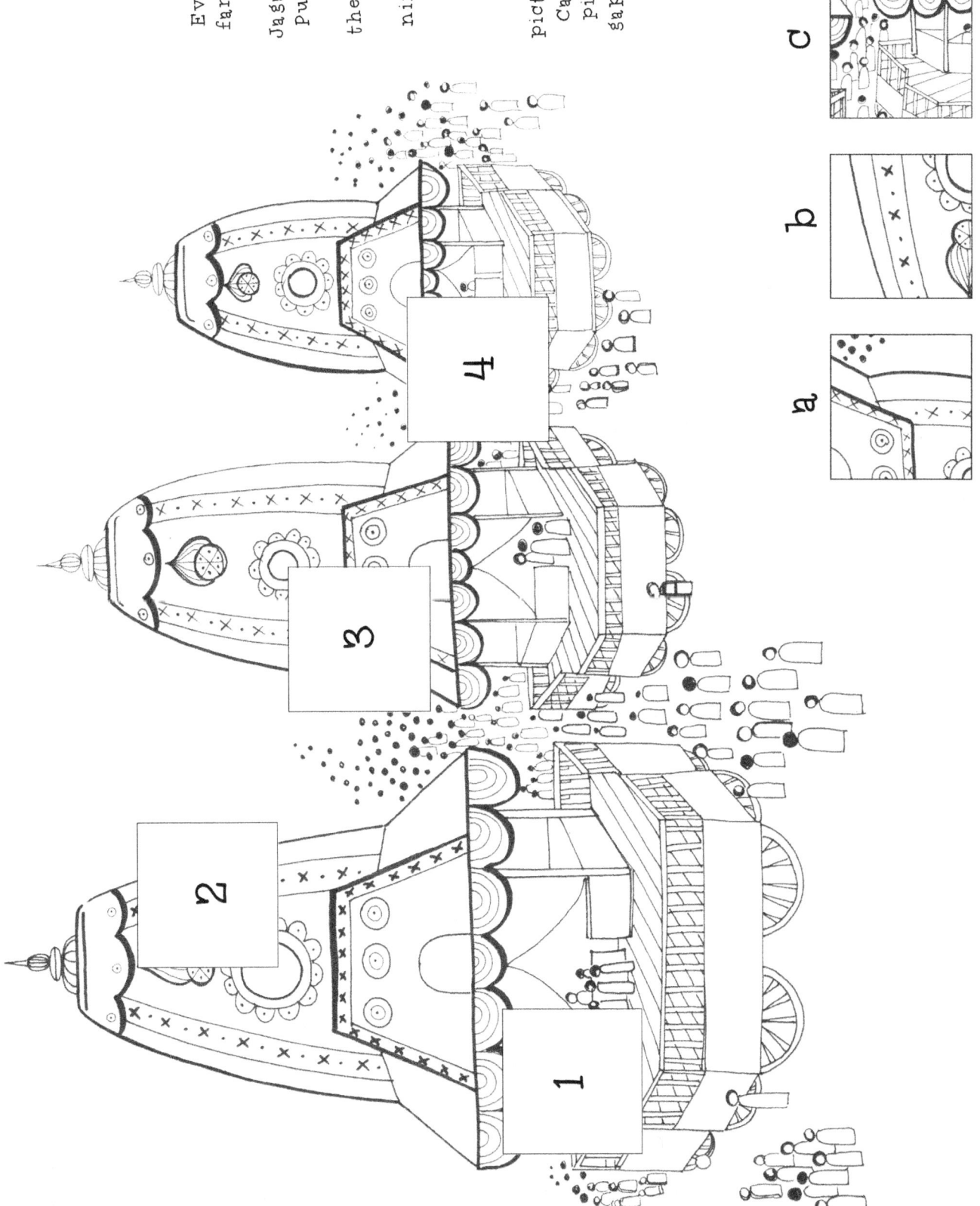

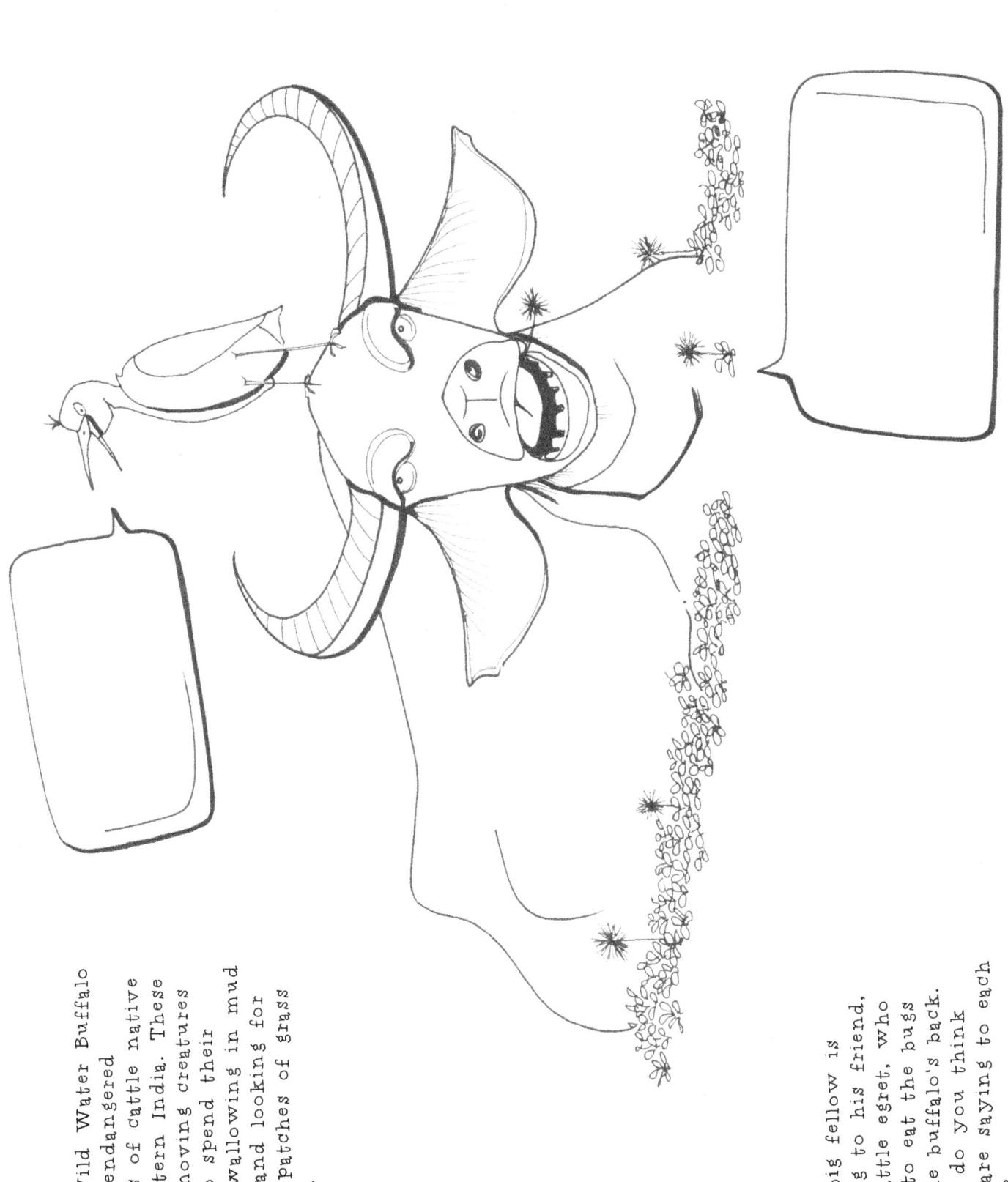

The Wild Water Buffalo is an endangered species of cattle native to Eastern India. These slow-moving creatures like to spend their days wallowing in mud pools and looking for tasty patches of grass to eat.

This big fellow is talking to his friend, the cattle egret, who likes to eat the bugs off the buffalo's back. What do you think they are saying to each other?

The Mahabodhi Temple in Bodh Gaya is one of the most important religious places for Buddhists. This temple is built on the spot where a Prince named Siddhartha became the Gautama Buddha.

Can you complete this picture of the temple by copying the shapes from the other side?

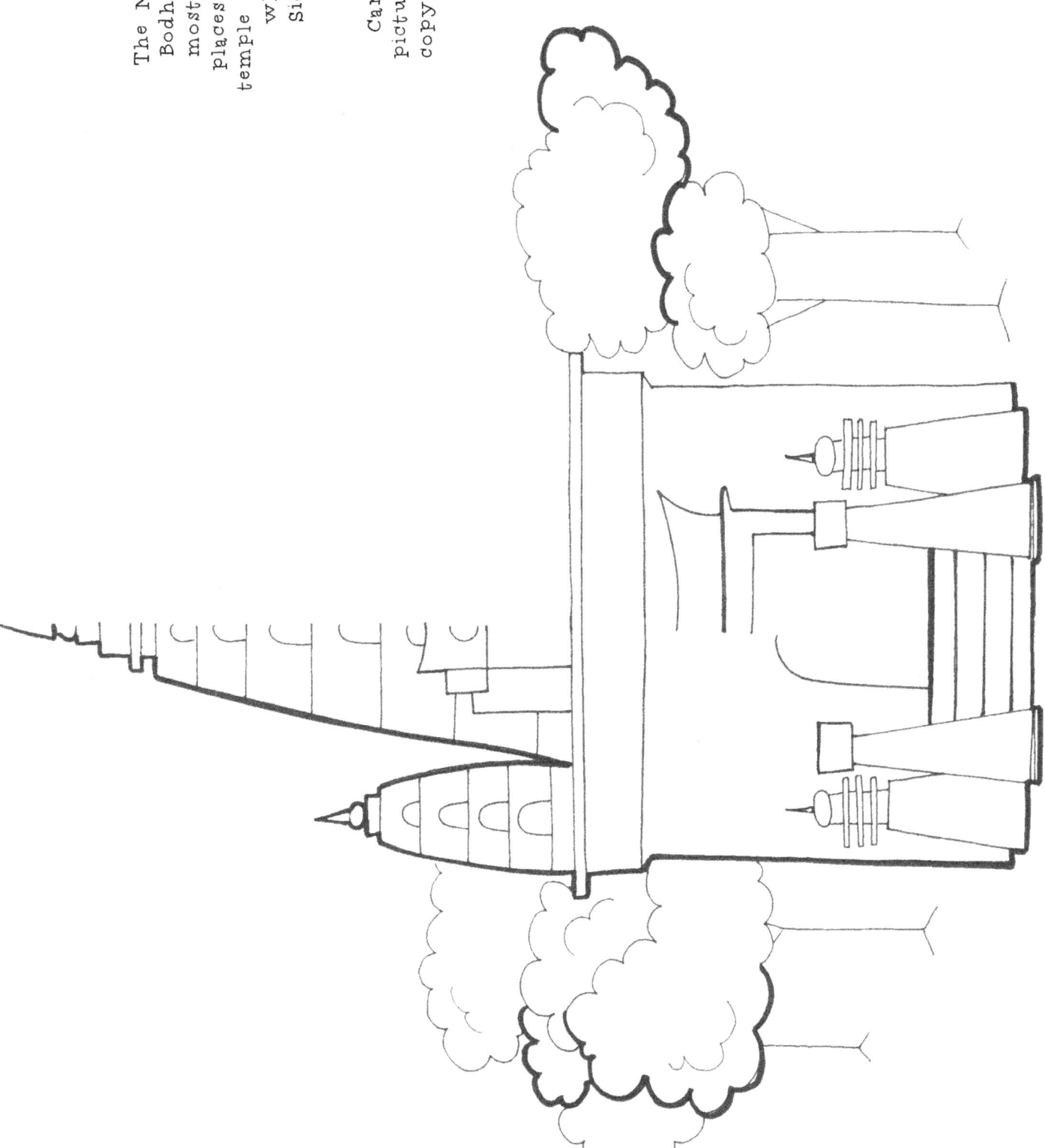

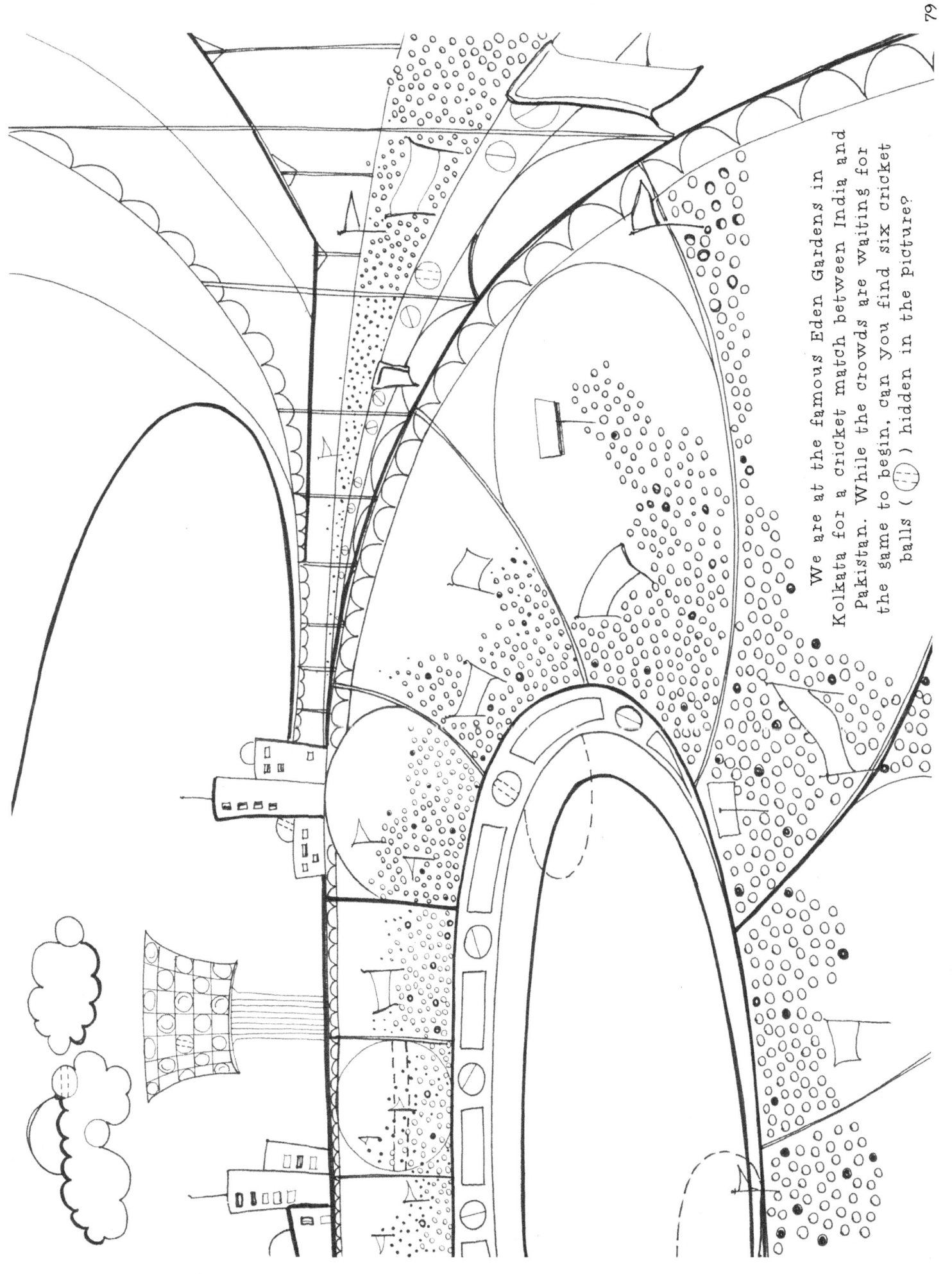

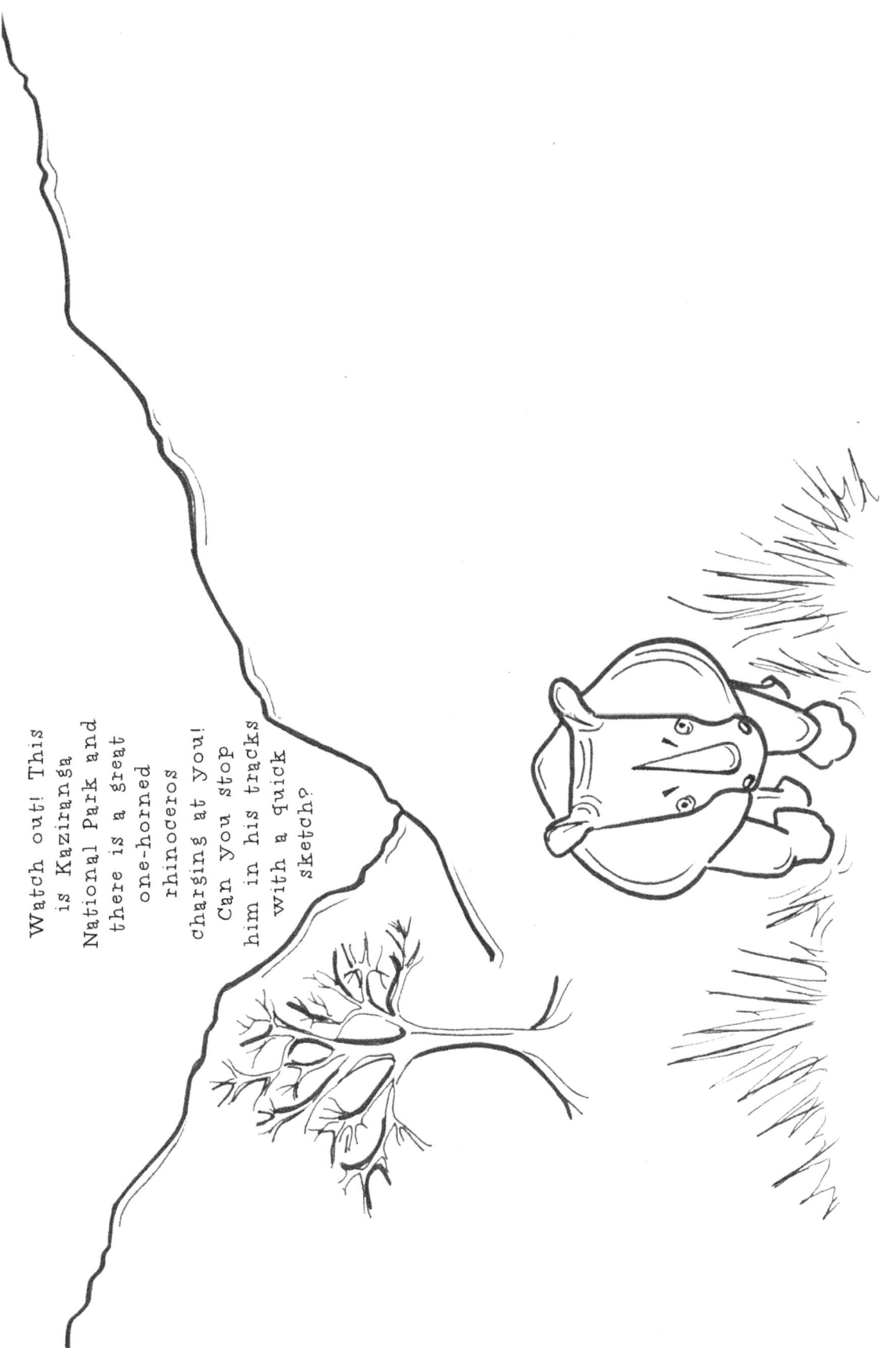

Watch out! This is Kaziranga National Park and there is a great one-horned rhinoceros charging at you! Can you stop him in his tracks with a quick sketch?

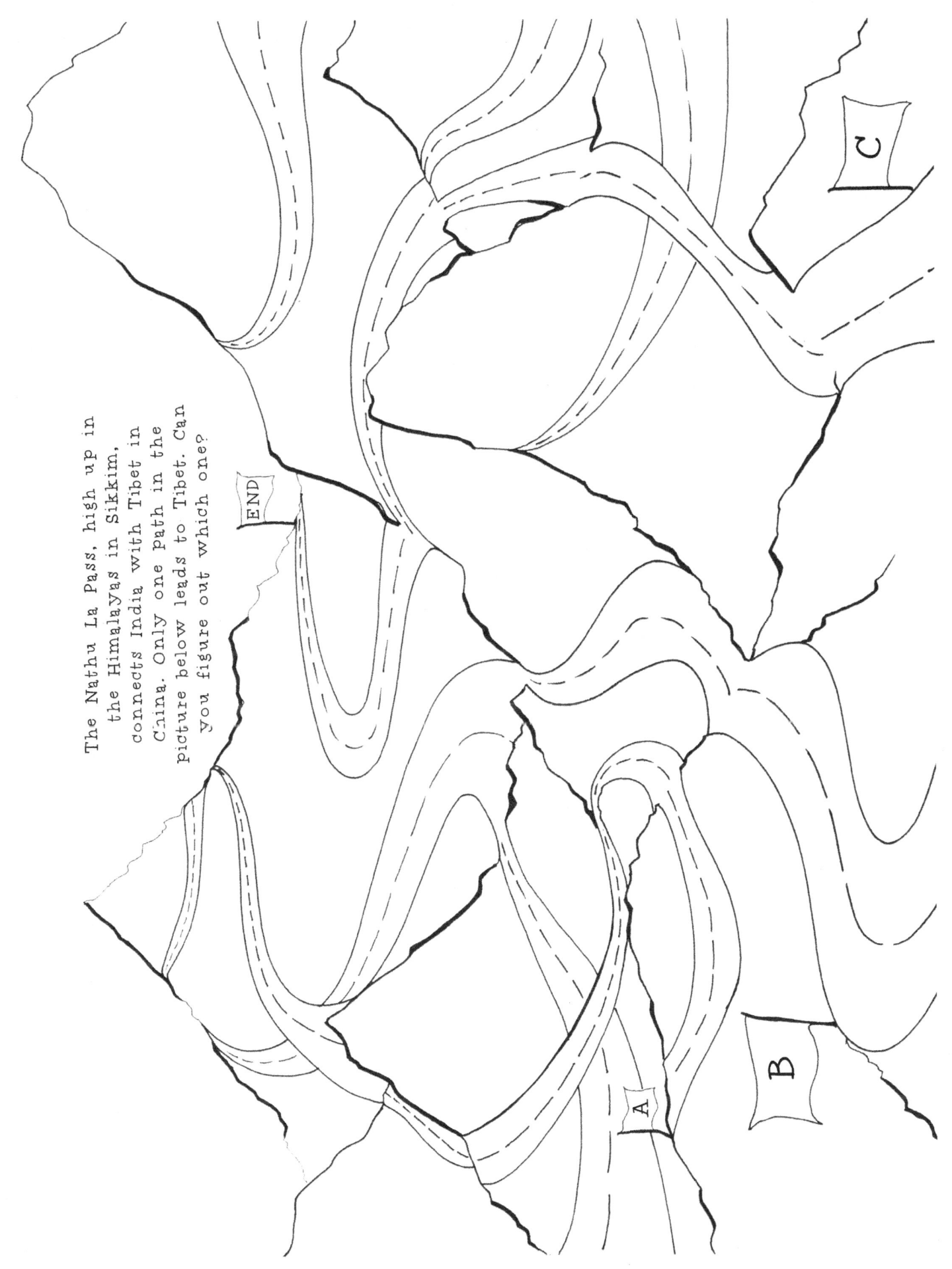

orange oakleaf

common red apollo

bhutan glory

yellow gorgon

kaiser-i-hind

The mountainous state of Sikkim is home to nearly 700 species of rare butterflies. We found five but they seem a bit incomplete. Can you copy the shapes from one side to the other as a mirror image to make these insects whole?

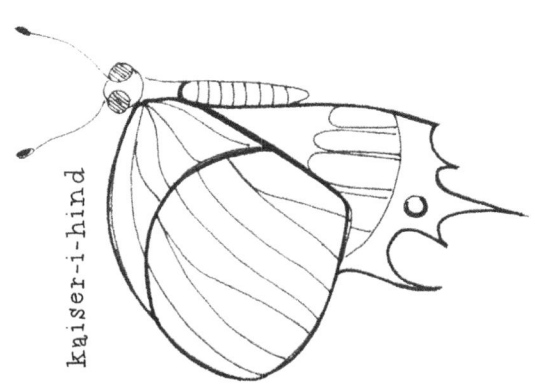
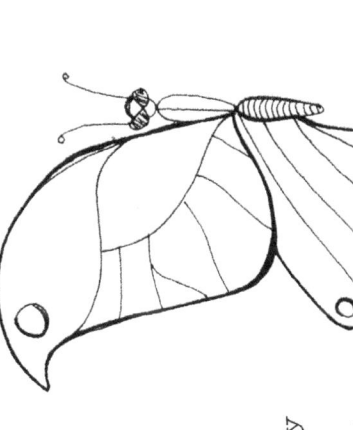

In rainy Meghalaya, we are collecting unique flowers called orchids, some of which are only found here. Only two of these are identical. Can you spot them?

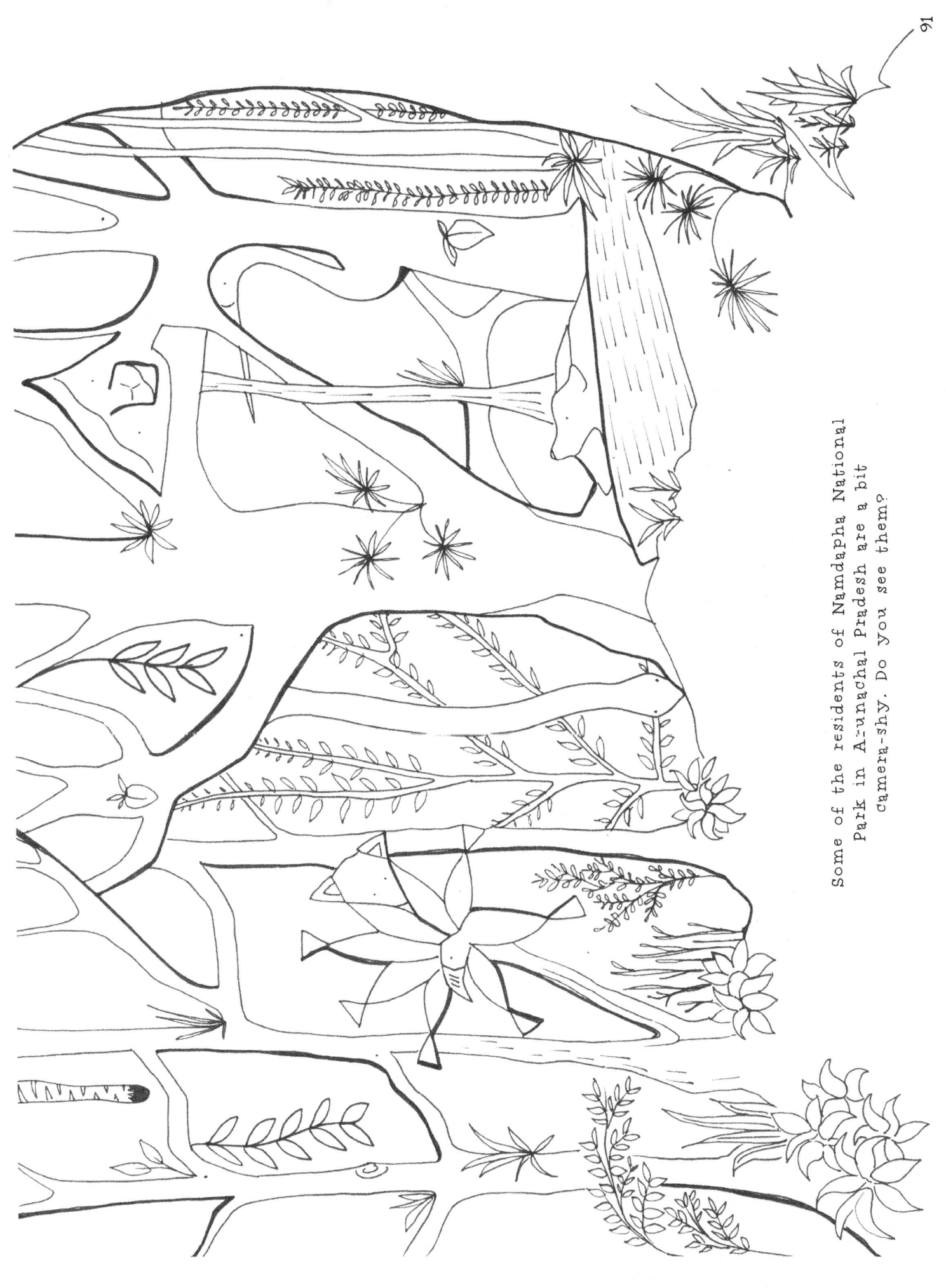

Some of the residents of Namdapha National Park in Arunachal Pradesh are a bit camera-shy. Do you see them?

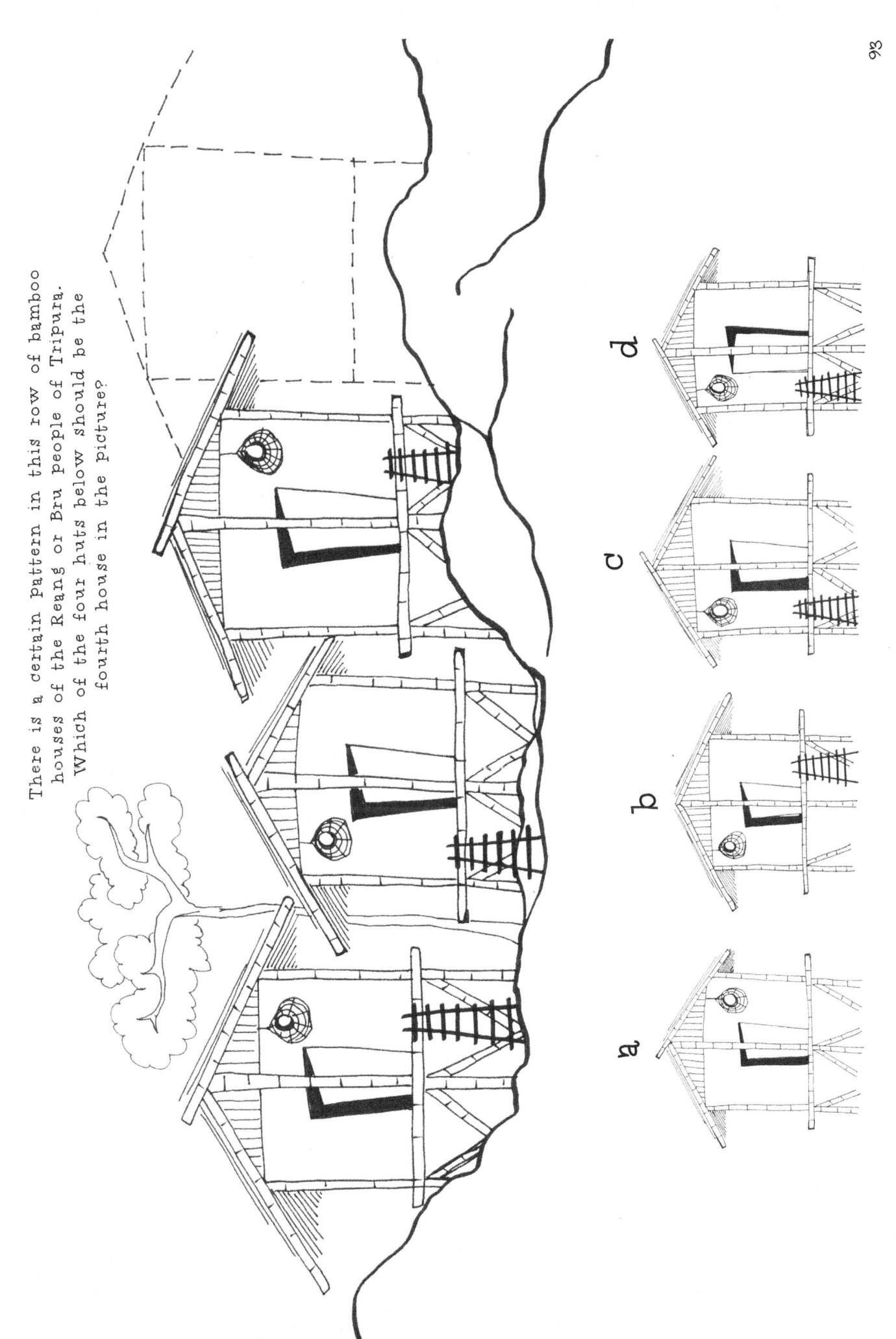

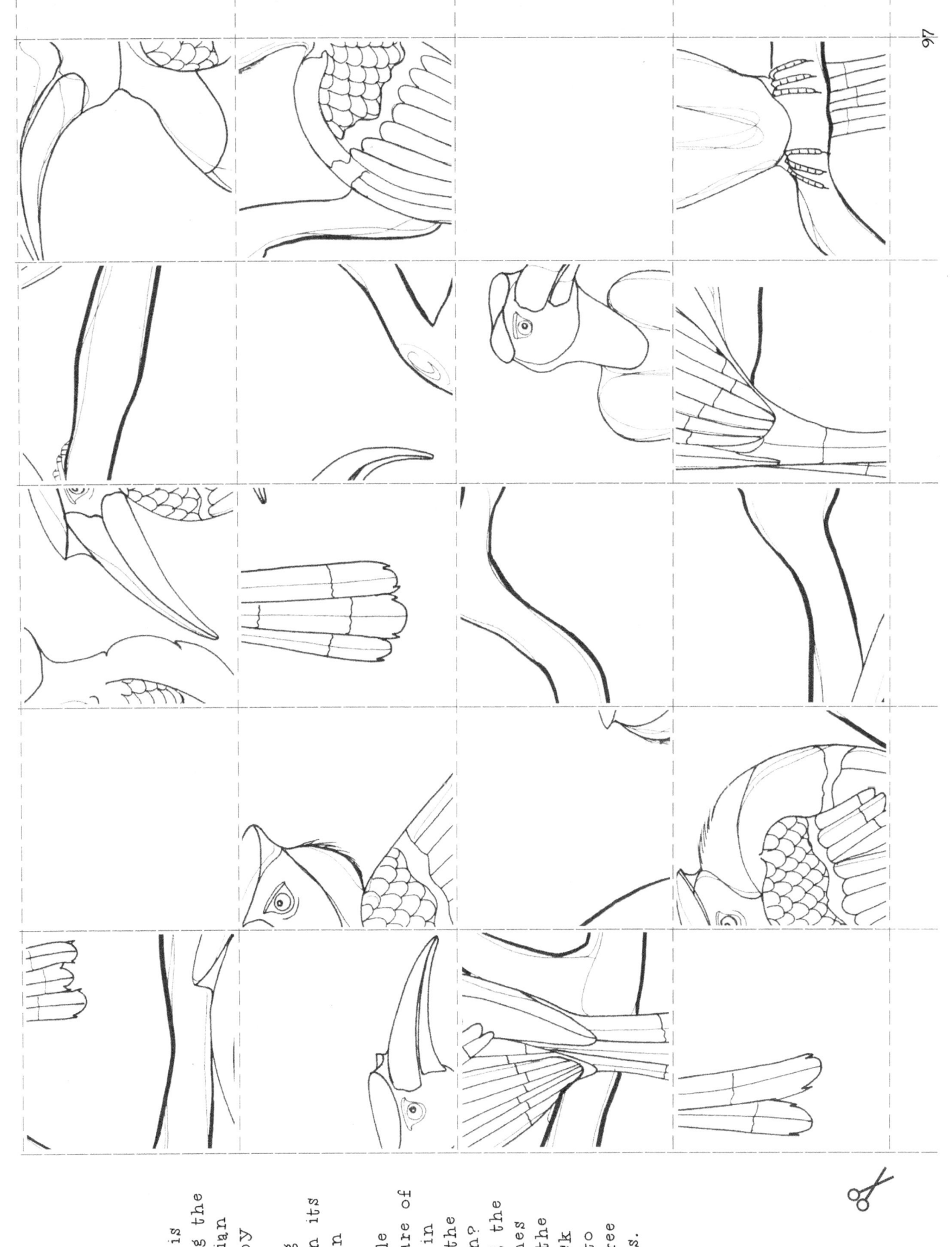

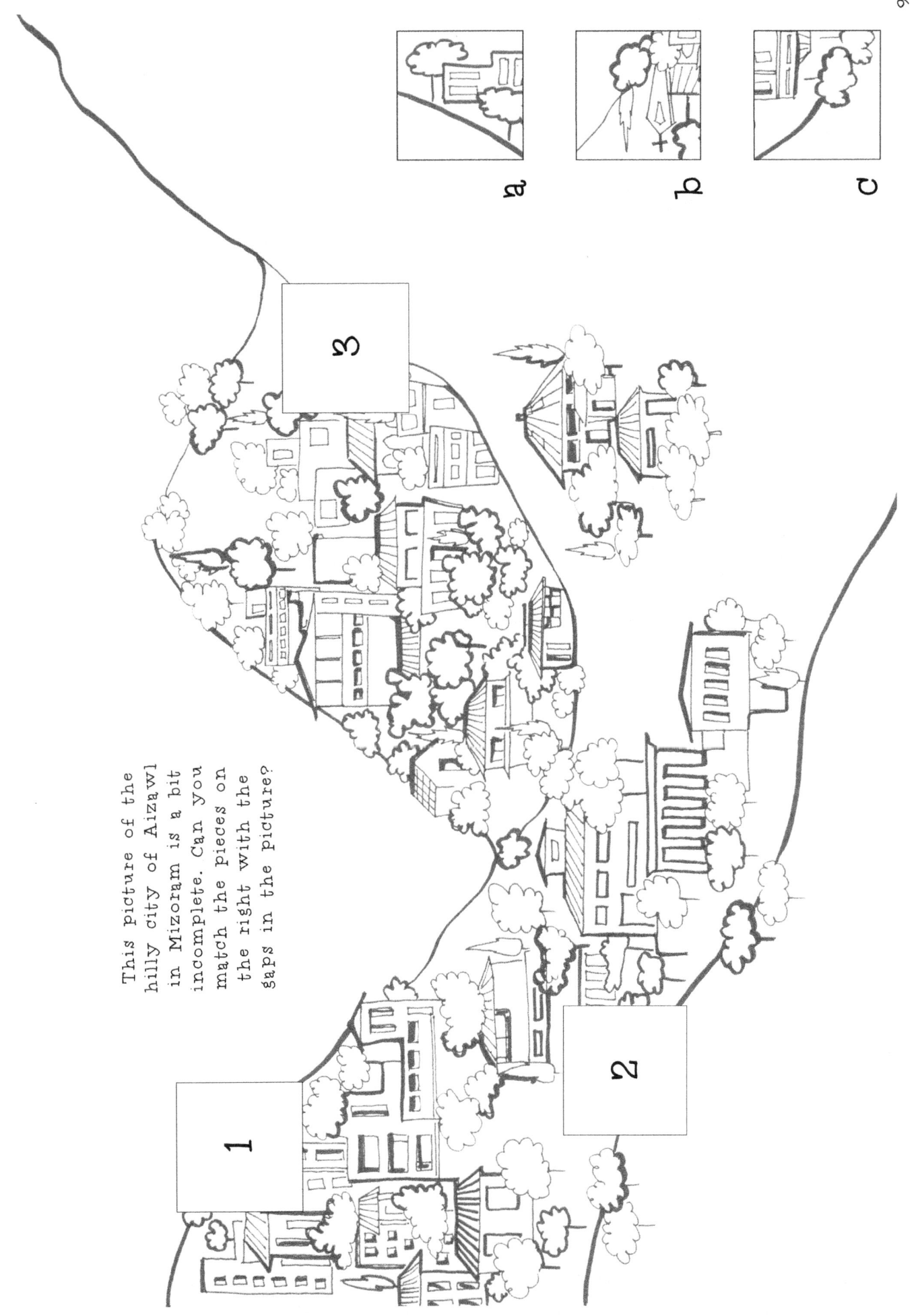

This shy sea mammal is found in the Andaman Sea. She spends most of her time eating sea grass and talking to her family in whistles and barks.

Can you figure out her name? Use the first letter of each of the objects in the boxes to spell out the word.

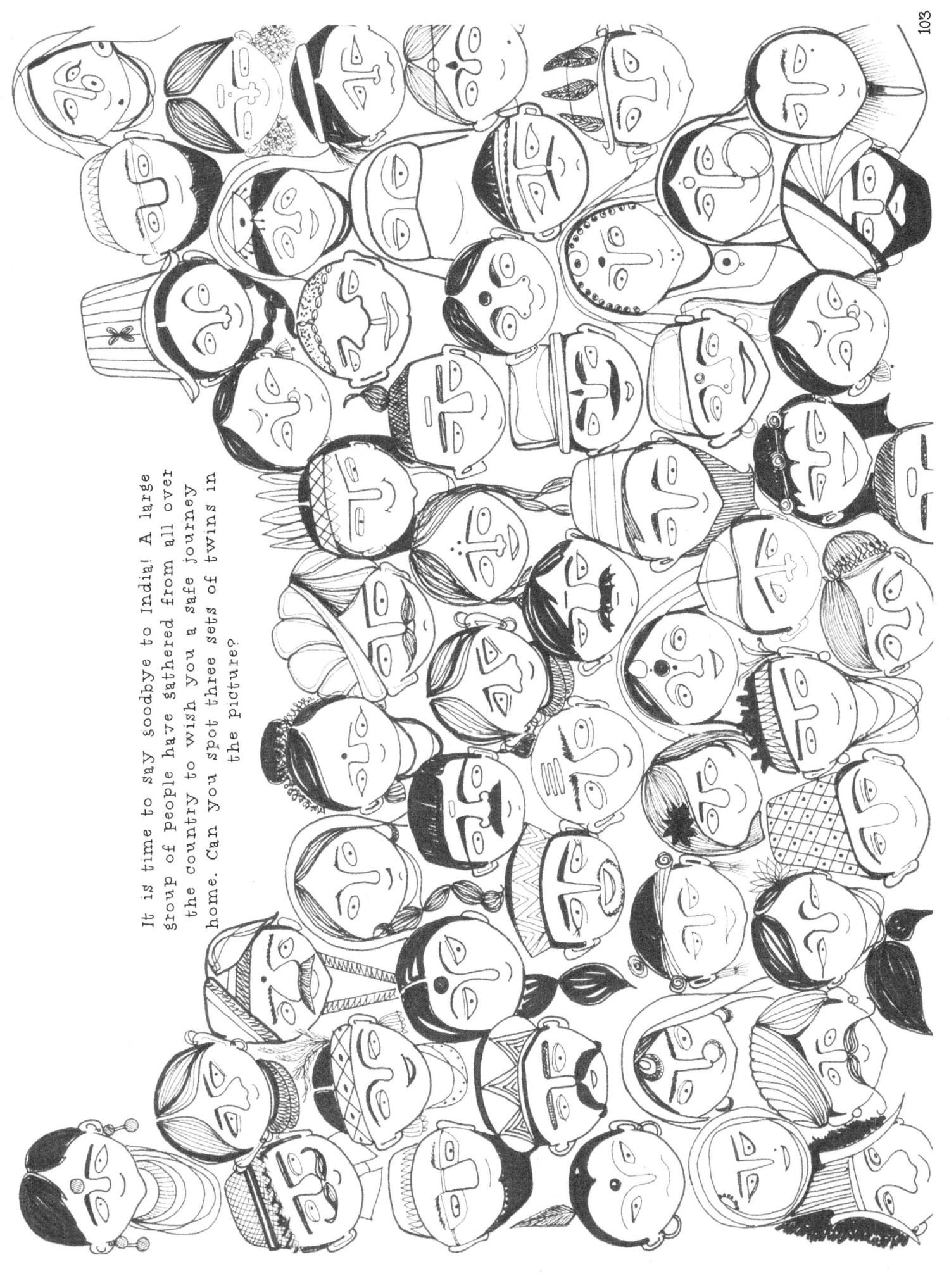

page 3

ANSWerS

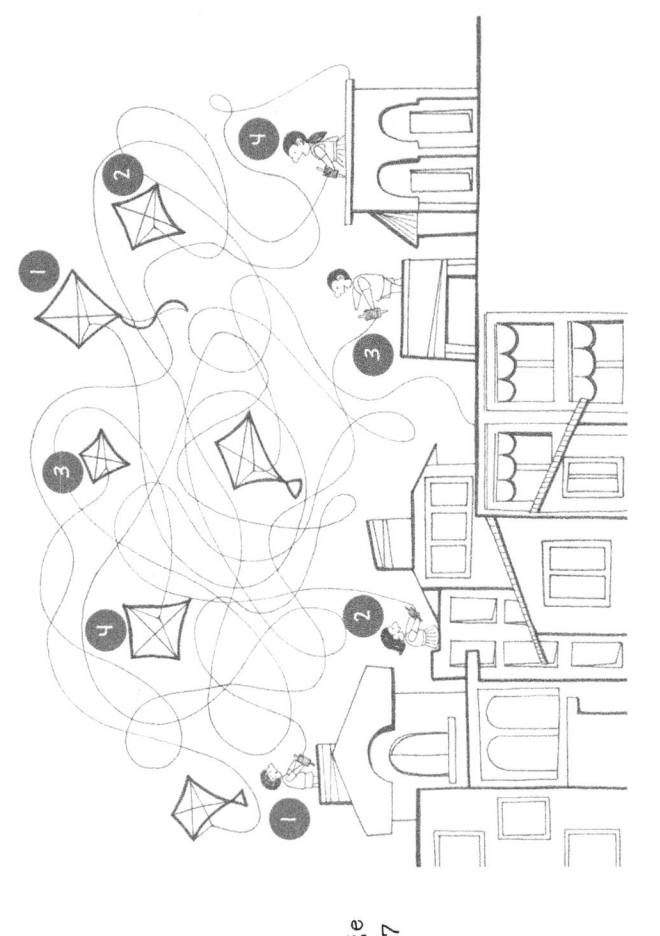

page 5

page 7

page 9

page 11

page 13

page 15

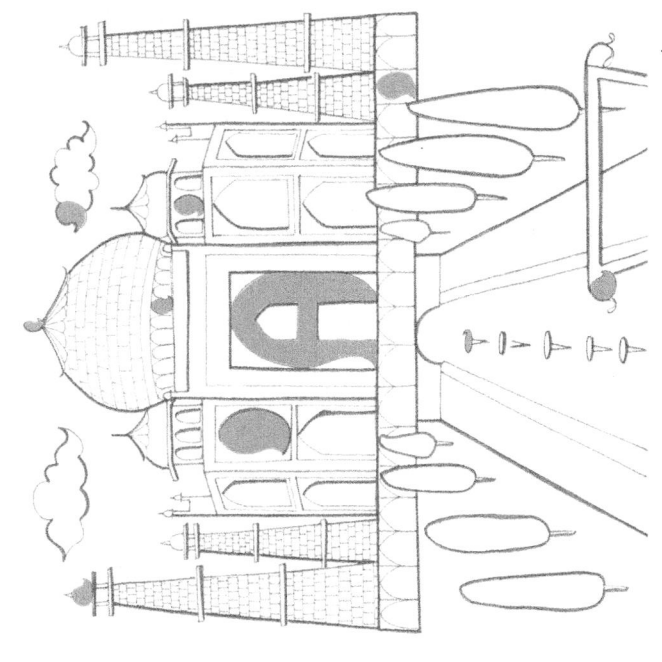

Page 17

Page 19

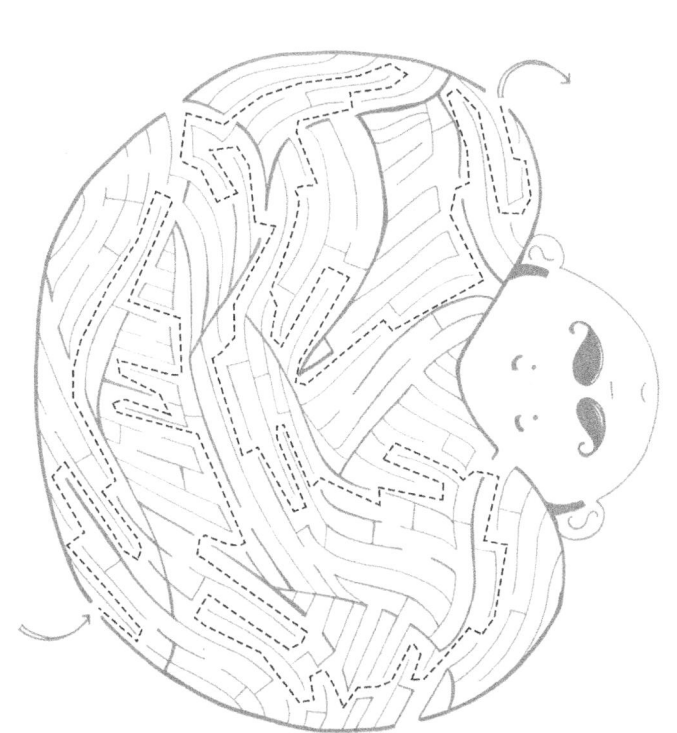

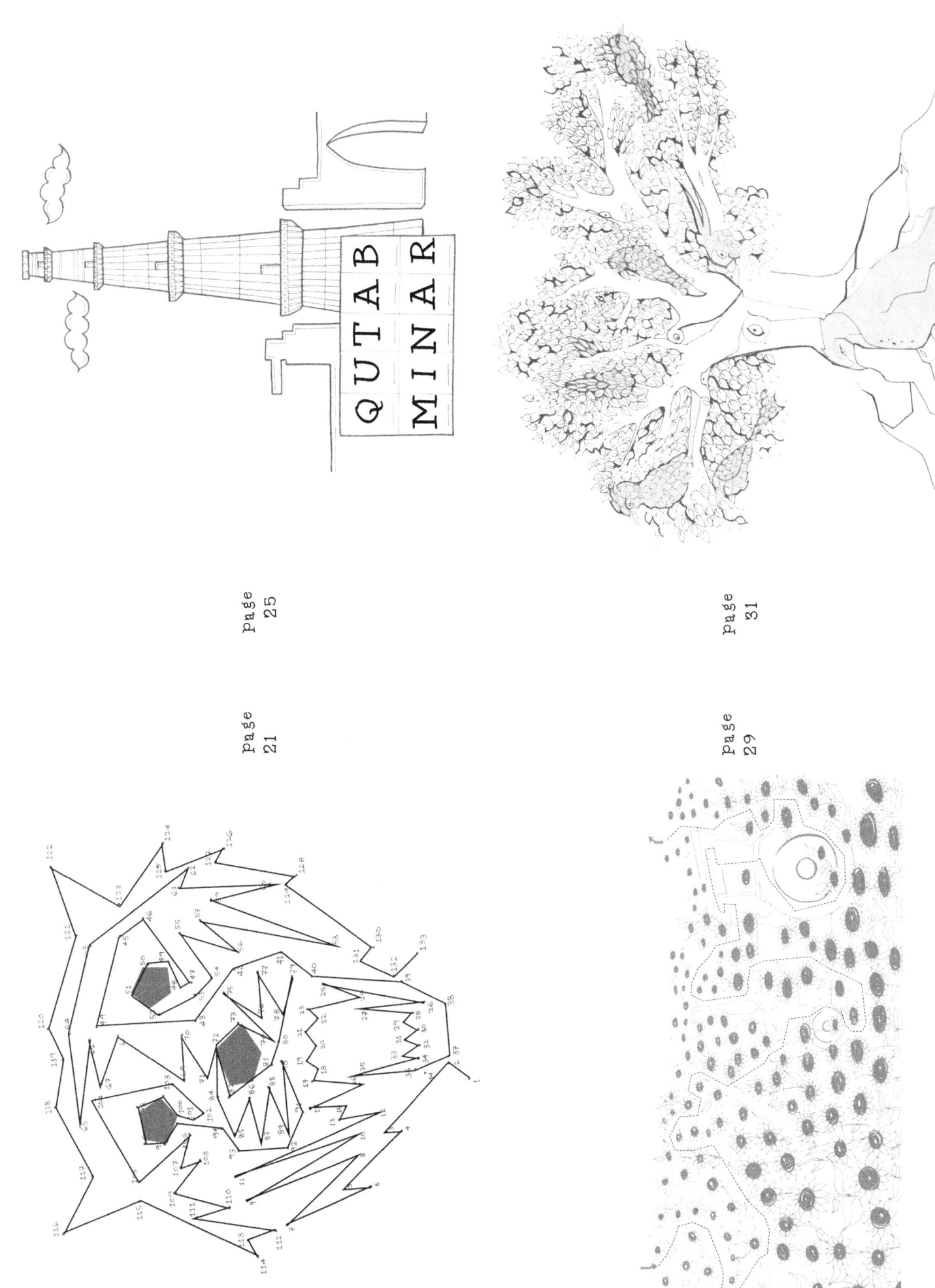

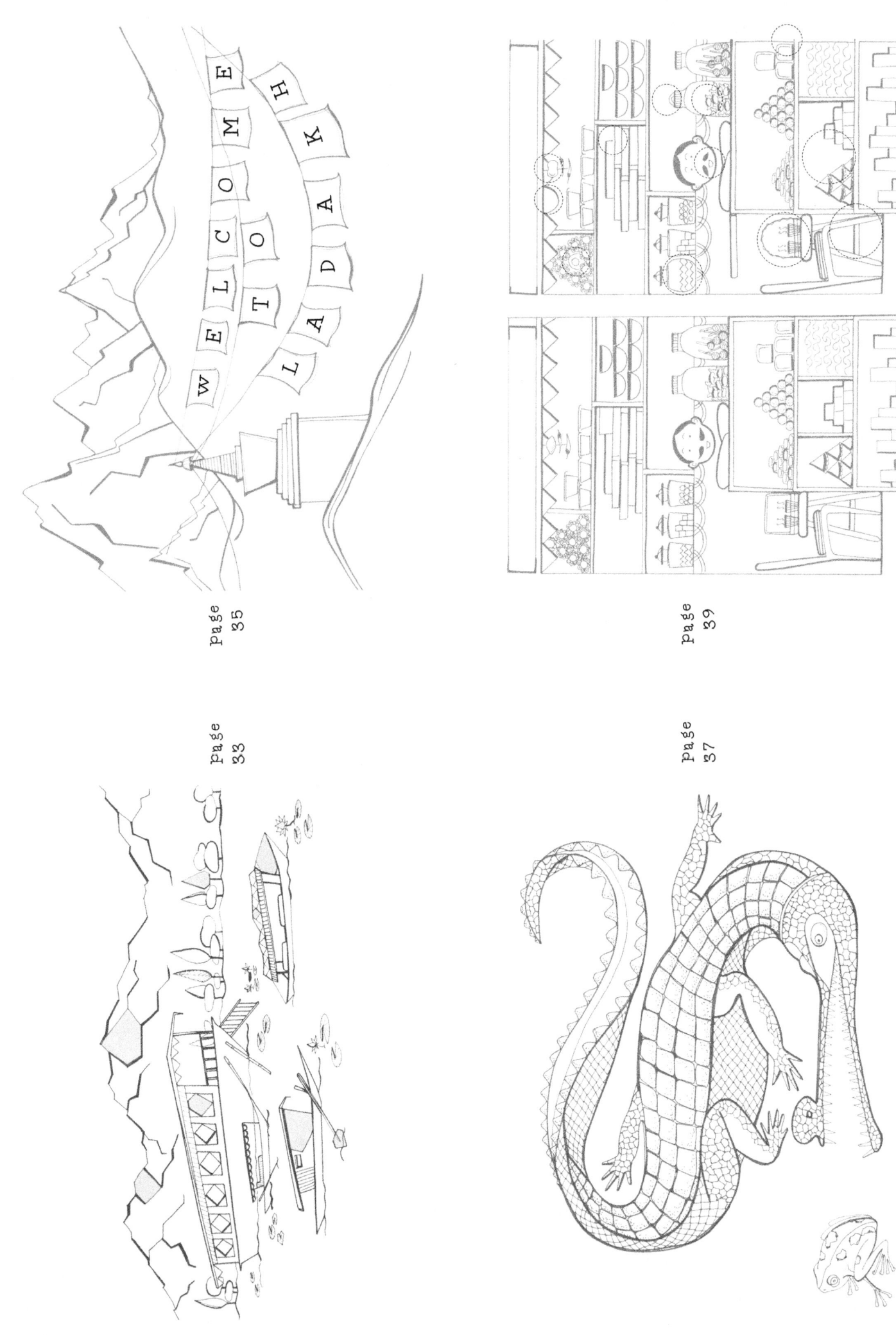

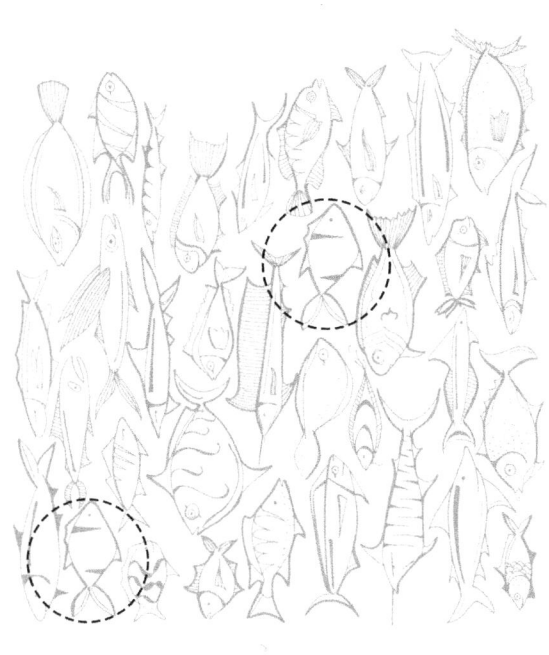

page 51

page 61

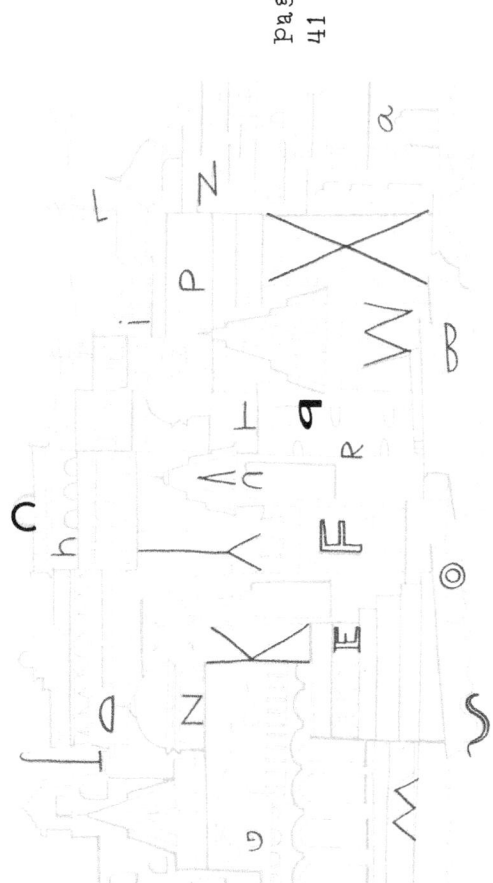

page 41

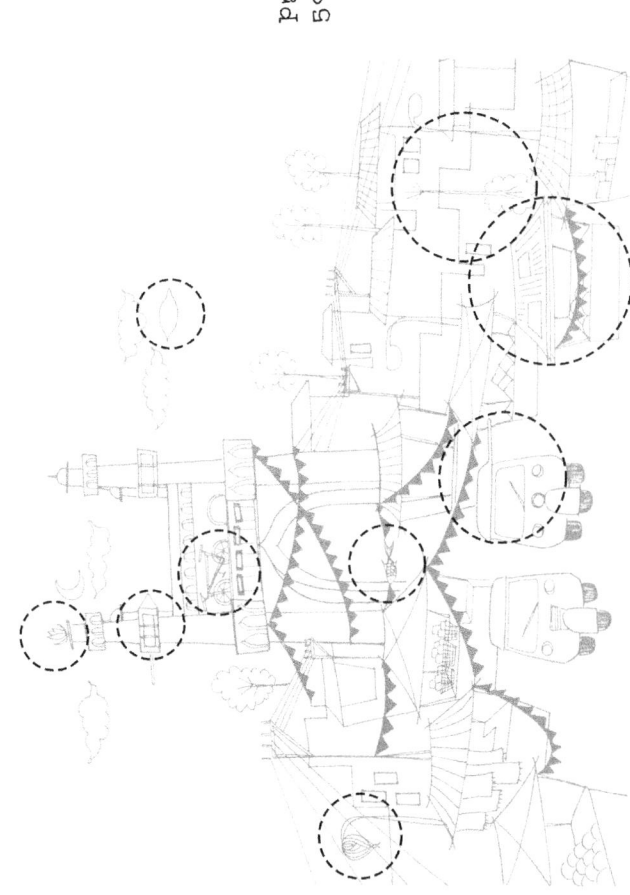

page 59

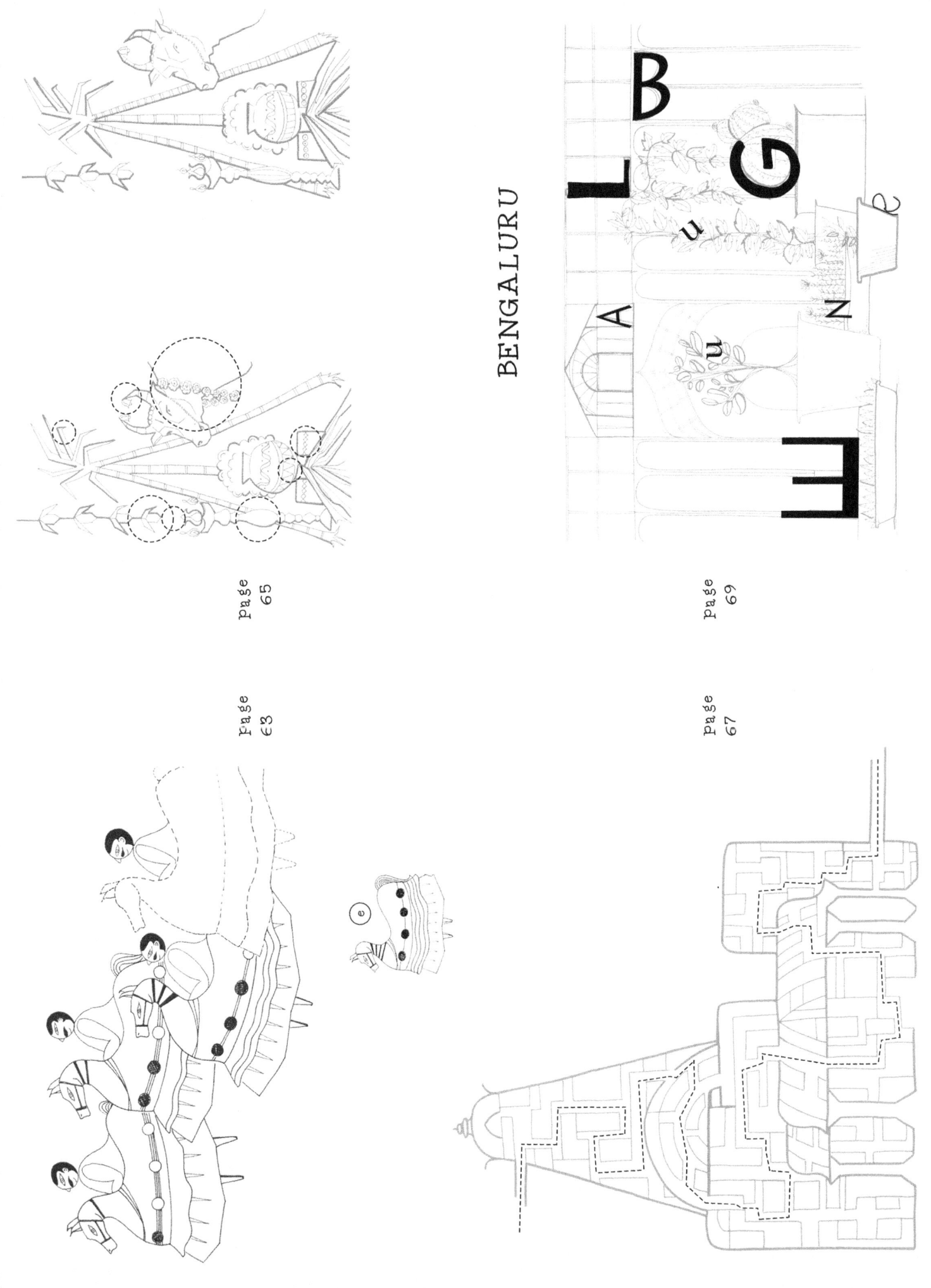

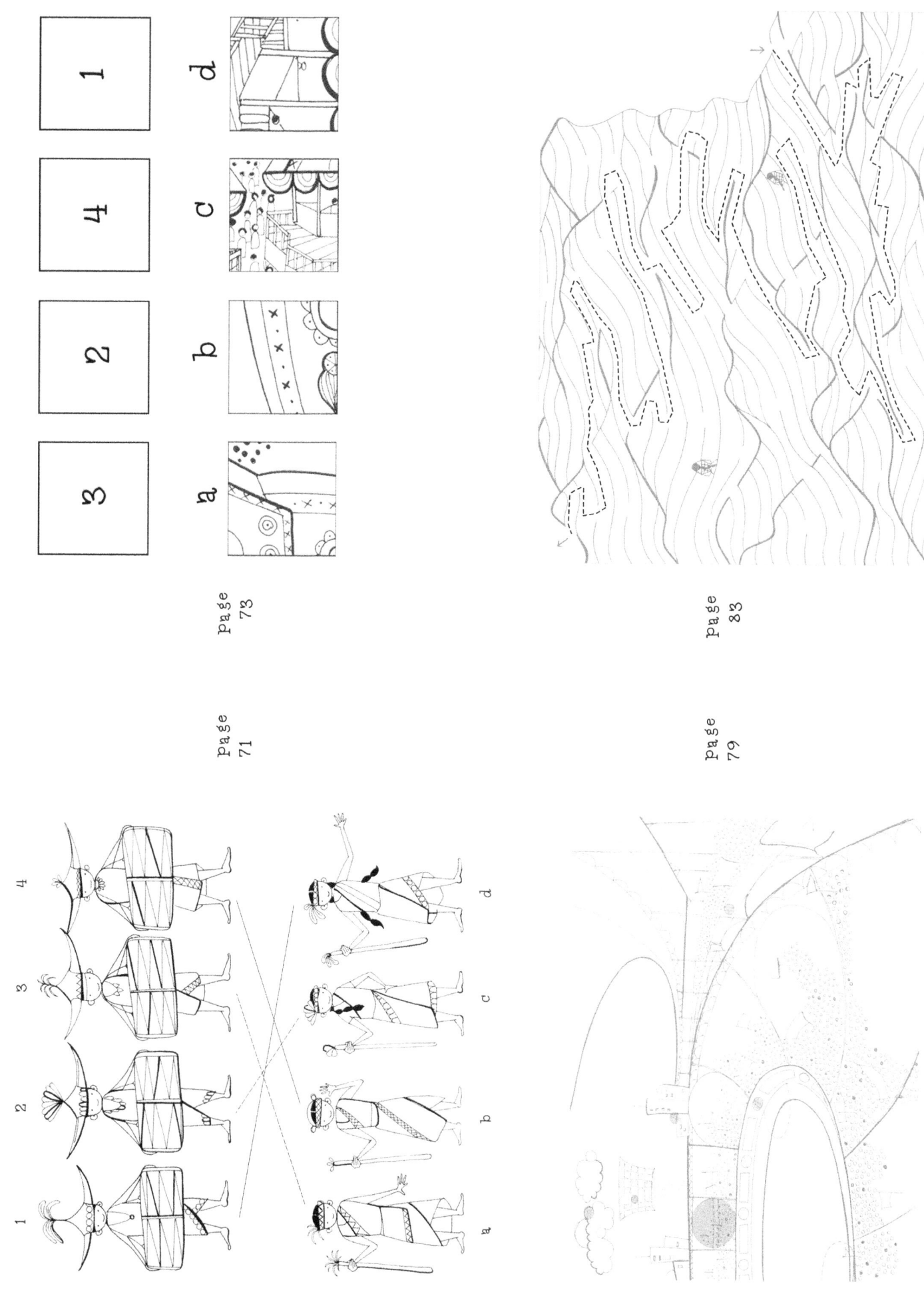

Page 85

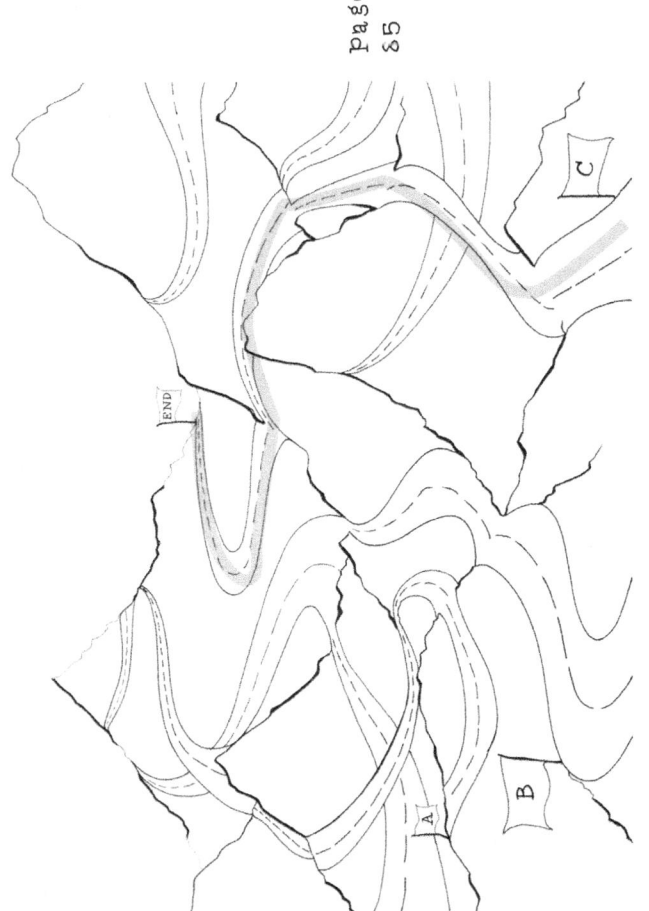

Page 89

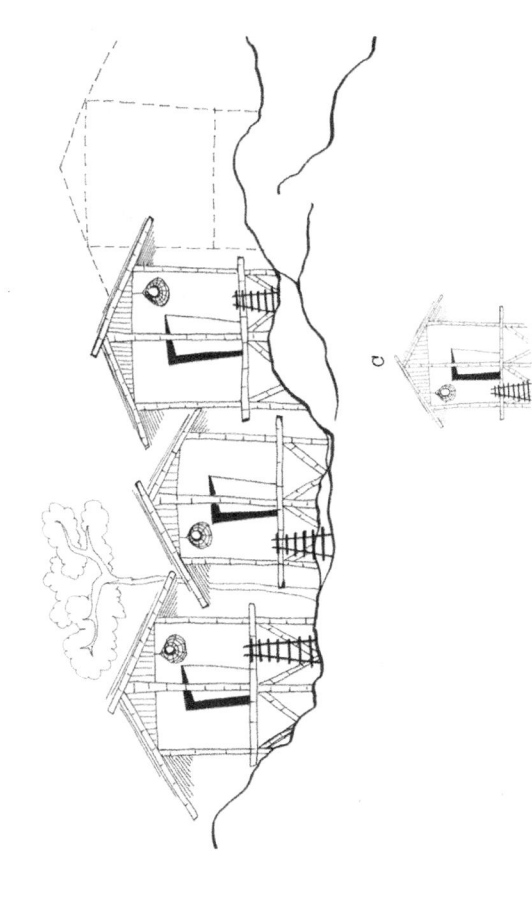

Page 91

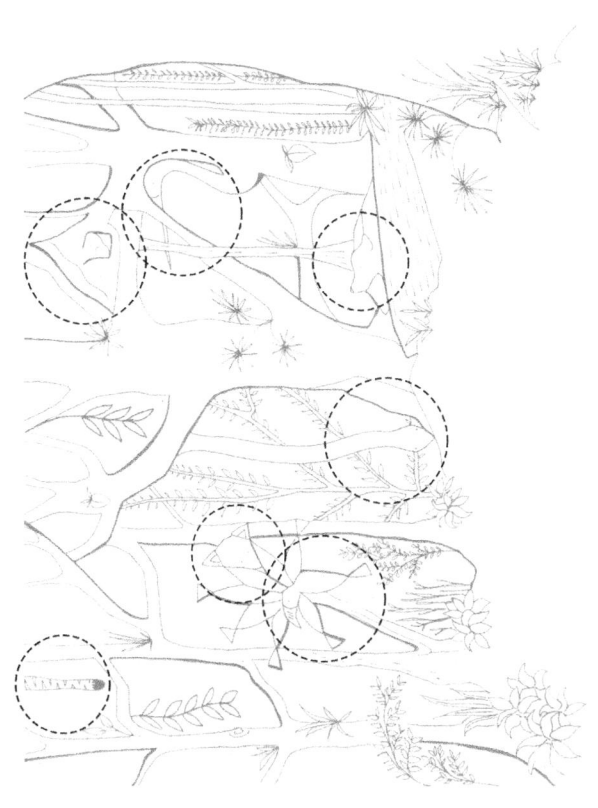

Page 93

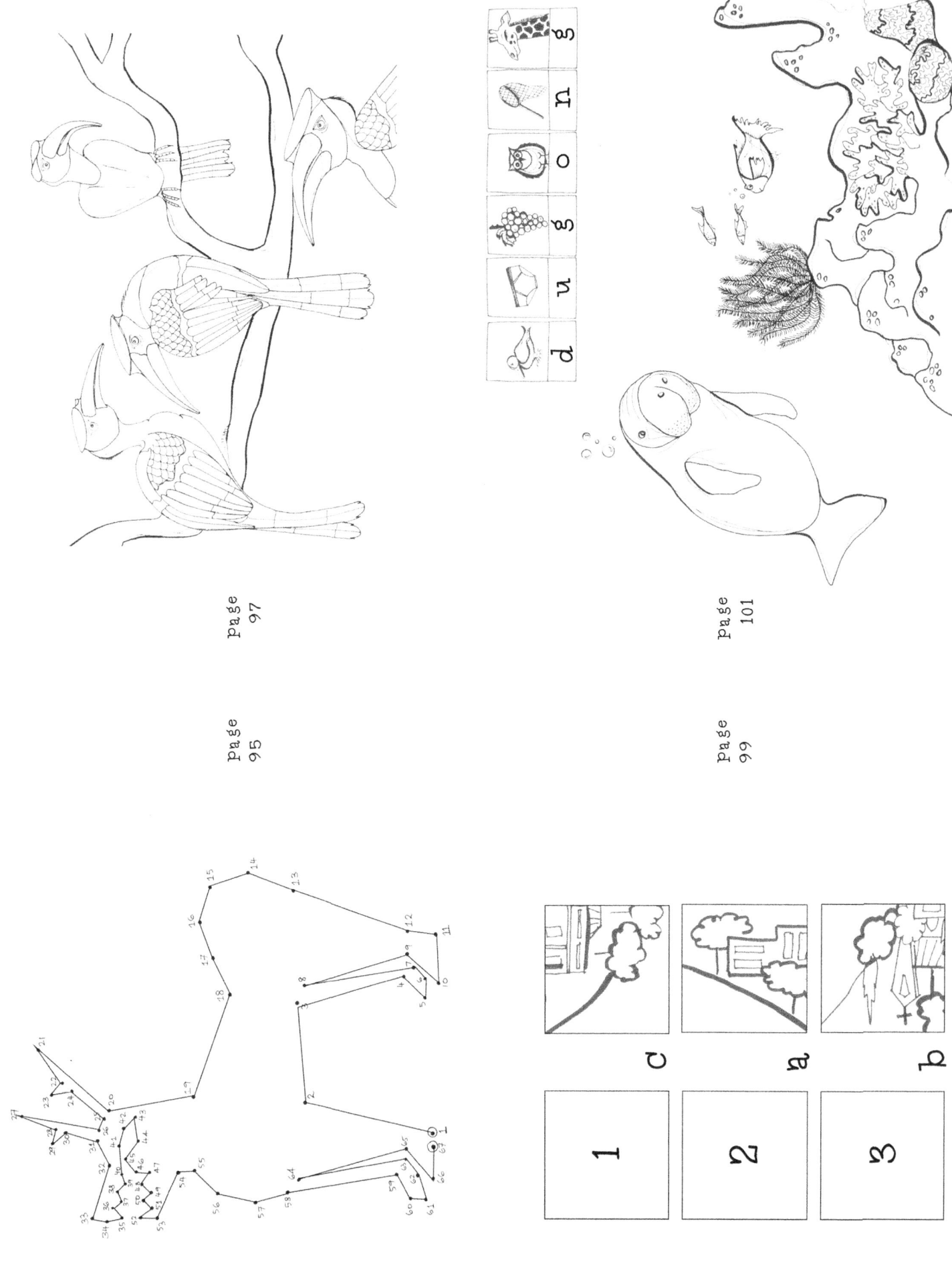

page 95

page 97

page 99

page 101

page 103

Made in the USA
Middletown, DE
20 February 2022